"A profound and beautifully crafted work of discovery by a pilot who flies with open eyes."

—William Langewiesche, international correspondent for *Vanity Fair*

"Rarely does a book about flying airplanes swoop gently into history, philosophy, geology, and science. This one does. And if you want to fly an airplane, *Prairie Sky* by Scott Olsen puts your hands, head, and heart at the controls. If you already fly and love it, and have never quite discovered the secrets of that love, then Olsen's narrative uncovers those secrets. Become young again. Fly this book."

—Clyde Edgerton, author of *The Floatplane Notebooks*

"In this soaring book, Scott Olsen offers up a twin paean to the beauty of flight and the gravitational pull of the upper Midwest. From the cockpit of a rented Cessna, Olsen flies us through history, epic weather, geology, human endeavor, and the pure, sometimes terrifying joy of being alive in a world of marvels. *Prairie Sky* is a lovingly chanted hymn to a place we thought we knew but in fact never probed from such height and with such depth."

—David Laskin, author of *The Children's Blizzard* and *The Family: Three Journeys into the Heart of the Twentieth Century*

"To understand why flying small airplanes above wide-open spaces is so compelling— and it is—one needs to grasp the intricacies of the intersection between earth and sky, a place where pilots spend their time while aloft and to which we devote our thoughts while earthbound. In his masterful, meditative, and authentic book, Scott Olsen maps patiently and precisely that middle ground, that space through which we pilots travel in our airplanes, blunt mechanical devices that give access, through Scott's brilliant prose, to that which is sublime around . . . and below us."

—Robert Goyer, editor-in-chief of *Flying*

"Scott Olsen's *Prairie Sky* may be about the author's flying adventures, but a mere book about flying it is not. Olsen frees us of Earth's surly bonds as we discover our home from a new perspective. His rich detail reads like an explorer's notebook, causing the reader to see their surroundings like never before. With *Prairie Sky*, Olsen reveals every pilot's biggest secret—flying is, above all, about the view."

—Ian Twombly, editor of *Flight Training*

Prairie Sky

Prairie Sky

A Pilot's Reflections on Flying
and the Grace of Altitude

W. Scott Olsen

University of Missouri Press   Columbia and London

Copyright © 2013 by
The Curators of the University of Missouri
University of Missouri Press, Columbia, Missouri 65201
Printed and bound in the United States of America
All rights reserved
5 4 3 2 1   17 16 15 14 13

Cataloging-in-Publication data available from the Library of Congress
ISBN 978-0-8262-2007-3

∞™ This paper meets the requirements of the
American National Standard for Permanence of Paper
for Printed Library Materials, Z39.48, 1984.

Cover design: Susan Ferber
Text design and composition: Jennifer Cropp
Printing and binding: Thomson-Shore, Inc.
Typefaces: Minon and Utopia

For my family

Flying at its best is a way of thinking.

—William Langewiesche, *Inside the Sky*

Contents

Prologue

Walking Chaucer

* *

Here is a question:

What must the angels think of the earth?

Imagine, for just a moment, the leap of their arrival. In the moment before, they are ethereal, weightless, timeless and light, the moral sparks of eternity. In the moment after, they have atomic weight. They have mass. They have capillaries and tympanum and knees. They have synapses that do and do not fire. When they inhale, they smell juniper or sage.

What must that moment be like, I wonder. To come suddenly into a body, into a physical world, and then be faced with Everest, Atlantic, Sequoia, Rift. Bearing whatever message, do they tremble in front of a prairie thunderstorm? What sense do they make of *le vent rouge*? What must that first gasp mean? Is the first emotion of the arrival humility? Fear? Awe? Gratitude?

We live on an unsteady planet.

Every day forward from the last Big Bang, the material that is us has been moving. Light-years in microseconds at first. Then slightly cooler. Then slightly slower. The gas cooled to dust. Gravity, the weakest force in the universe, arrested everything. Dust collected onto other dust. Stars became stars. Galaxies lit up the void. Planets got themselves together. The whole inexorable dance. Dark matter. Radio waves. Creation versus Entropy. The tug and pull of being.

Movement became everything. Animate means alive and it means able to move. Temperature is a measure of movement. Absolute zero, the coldest possible temperature, is the point where all molecular motion stops. The hottest temperature is the "come hither" look of the beautiful other.

Our landscape seems stable, the grocery store remains where we left it yesterday, but we know it is not. Underneath our highways, our lawns, our soccer fields and oceans, we live on a sea of molten rock, a fluid in motion, thrusting and strike-slipping our tectonic plates around the globe. The air above us roils from one season to the next. Tides rise and fall. Sparks turn to fire and the wholesale exchange of matter into energy.

The magnetic poles wander around their landscapes, sometimes as much as eighty-five kilometers in one day. More than once, the whole magnetosphere has slipped the whole way 'round. More slowly, but inevitably, the planet wobbles—the geographic North Pole points toward Polaris, and then does not. The earth orbits. The earth spins. Every middle school student learns about the Coriolis effect and the deflected paths of storms.

Our language is filled with the ways the earth resists the stationary. Mud slide. Rock slide. Downpour. Torrent. Tremor. Cataract. Conflagration. Inferno. Blaze. Tornado. Hurricane. Gust front. Blizzard. Earthquake. Fault. Riptide. Whirlpool. Maelstrom. Volcano. Flood. Cold front. Storm. Tsunami. Cyclone. Monsoon. And our stories carry the tremulous weight of the gods.

In Norwegian, *Tordenvær,* literally "thunderweather," or better as "thunderstorm," is the sound of Tor (in English, Thor), the god of thunder, and his hammer. Thunder is rare in Norway, and the sound of it rattles marrow.

In the Caribbean, Jurakán was a god of the Taínos, who lived on what are now Puerto Rico, the Dominican Republic, and Haiti, the Leeward and Windward Islands. He had a temper, like Zeus and Thor. The Spaniards heard about him and called him "huracán" and from there "hurricane."

In the book of Job, God speaks from a whirlwind. *Then the LORD answered Job out of the whirlwind and said, "Who is this that darkens counsel by words without knowledge? Now gird up your loins like a man, and I will ask you, and you instruct Me! Where were you when I laid the foundation of the earth?"*

In West Africa, the Hausa people refer to a particular wind as *iska zahi,* the hot wind. *Iska,* which means "wind," also means "ghost." It also means "spirit." It means the movement of the air has meaning.

Beyond the gods, this same Harmattan wind is the source of the famous *le vent rouge*—the red wind. Red quartz from the African deserts is carried aloft, and then north, and then falls in rain across southern Italy, France, and Spain. There are stories about rain gutters along the streets of Marseille running maroon after rain that blows in from the Sahara across the Mediterranean. There are stories of *le vent rouge* turning the snowfields of Scandinavia pink.

There is a proverb in Japanese—a list of the four most fearful things: *jishin, kaminari, kaji, oyaji.* Earthquakes, lightning, fires, and father.

In German, *Donner* and *Blitzen* are not just cute reindeer. They are thunder and lightning. *Donnerwetter* means "thunderstorm," and it is also what you say when what you mean is "damn it all."

Movement is everything. The slow and subtle movement of waves grinds rock into sand. A molten layer bubbles and shifts the cooler crust. Plates collide and create the Himalayas. Plates pull apart, ram back together, pull apart, ram back together, pull apart again, and eventually make an Atlantic Ocean. The Gulf Stream carries heat from St. Croix to Rannoch Moor. In the North Atlantic as well as the Southern Ocean, deep water is formed—dense cold water sinking into deep basins. This deep water creeps along the ocean floors, mixing and warming, finally rising to start it all over again. The great engine that keeps us alive.

The great engine also smacks us down. If this moment, the moment you are reading this sentence, is an average moment, there are a bit more than two thousand thunderstorms hammering the planet. Two thousand cumulonimbus clouds, anvil shaped at the top. Two thousand cells or supercells. Each of them dropping hail, wind, rain. Each of them announced by a gust front. A few of them birthing tornadoes.

If this day is an average day, lightning will strike more than three million times.

If today is a summer day, there are anywhere from five to forty large-incident fires burning in the United States. One hundred acres or more in timber. Three hundred acres or more in grassland.

If today is usual, ordinary, unspectacular and mundane, the earth will quake and move its shell fifty-five times. More than 20,000 times a year, every year, the plates buckle and shift. In 2005, 13,917 out of the 30,478 recorded quakes were 4.0 to 4.9. Of the total, 864 were listed as "no magnitude." Ten were magnitude 7.0 to 7.9. Only 1 was 8.0 or higher. In 2005, 82,364 people were killed by the moving earth.

The plates press against each other. The plates move apart. The Indian Plate pressing against the Eurasian Plate creates the Himalayas. The Australian Plate pressing against both the Indian and Eurasian Plates, at a place called the Burma Subplate, moves under water. On a completely unusual day in 2004, it moved a lot. Tsunami. A pressure wave in the ocean where it was displaced by the moving earth. A pressure wave, moving outward, reaching continental shelves and then beaches, 227,898 people dead from just this one event on the beaches of Indonesia, Sri Lanka, India, Thailand, Somalia, Myanmar, the Maldives, Malaysia, Tanzania, the Seychelles, Bangladesh, South Africa, Kenya. The passports of the dead included the whole world. And beyond the dead, there was horrifying damage. Indonesia. Thailand. India. Sri Lanka. Malaysia. Myanmar. Bangladesh. Maldives.

Reunion Island. Seychelles. Madagascar. Mauritius. Somalia. Tanzania. Kenya. Oman. South Africa. Australia.

Movement is everything. It can smack us dead. It defines our life.

What must the angels think when they arrive and their physical eyes see thunderstorm, cliff face, a miniature rose? Move, they think. Keep going. There are so many stories, and my time is short. Be ready.

I have a dog named Chaucer.

A tricolor collie, he looks at me, his long nose resting between his legs on the wood of our back porch, and wonders when we are going to leave. His desire is as plain as it is profound. He wants nothing more than to head out, to rush into the world, to see what is new and what has changed. Today, he knows, is a fine day for a walk. Today is a perfect day to visit the stories once again.

Sitting on the porch, a cup of coffee in my hands, I see beyond him the springtime prairie of North America unfolding uninterrupted until it fades over the curve of the earth. We live in a border town: between Minnesota and North Dakota; between lake country and high desert; between dust storm and blizzard. Between a summer light so gentle you swear you can rest your head on the air to sleep and a winter darkness so cold you swear you can trace the orbit of electrons in every breath. Border towns are edge places, meeting places, and there are days when it seems the best thing to do is sit quietly on a porch and watch the universe come visit. The sun and then the Milky Way orbit overhead. The water in the ground moves north toward Hudson Bay. In the yard beyond the porch this season we have seen the ordinary sparrow and nuthatch, killdeer and cowbird, robin and barn swallow, as well as sometimes a red-tailed hawk and, more rarely, a large owl we have not been able to identify. Ash trees. Maple trees. Evergreens. Two apple trees, their fruit from last year stored in our freezer for baking still to come—the warm smell of hot springtime apple pie. We have seen and talked with neighbors as well as strangers, people at work and children at play. It would be easy to sit here, almost grotesquely comfortable, with coffee and collie and simply watch the show and believe in deep ideas.

But today is a fine day for a walk. Today is a perfect day to make that pilgrimage once more, to leave the home in search of something troubling and something sacred, to visit the places we know as well as the ones we do not and smile when the world is larger than our ability to imagine it. Chaucer, of course, is named for the author of *The Canterbury Tales,* the first great travel story in English. You're on the road, his Innkeeper said. Tell me a story. And if it's a good one, we will all buy you dinner.

Exploration, said Apsley Cherry Gerard, is the physical expression of intellectual passion. Every good impulse is an impulse outward. Tell me a travel story? Chaucer gets up, stretches his forelegs and then his hind legs, and looks at me. Waiting. Wondering. Wishing. Let's go, he thinks.

Leaving is really his only question. He knows he will be fed. He knows he has shelter. He knows he has people to scratch his ears and rub his sides and tell him he is an astonishingly good-looking dog. And he knows we *will* leave. He knows that every day I will gather my cap, retie my laces, and head toward the back door. Together we will walk the circuit we've come to know as intimately as our own desire—the streets, the park, the pond, the river shore—but he does not know when. It could be morning, twilight, full-dark midnight. We do not wait for clear weather, so it could be windstorm, blizzard, summer heat. Every day his eyes watch me, looking for the signs that now, now is when we will go. Now is when we will see how the world has changed since yesterday, listening for each small new story. Now is when the old story gets told again. He lives his days in anticipation of departure, waiting for that heart-leap joy in the moment of setting out. And so do I. There are new stories in the world. It's time to get going.

Destination has nothing to do with the joy of travel. Destination is accomplishment and rest. The dance to get there, however, is everything. The journey is where the stories come from. Destination is the place where you tell them. And it does not matter if the excursion is the first ascent of an unnamed peak in a badly mapped wilderness or a familiar walk with a happy dog—there is as much of the universe in every leaving.

So three miles, more or less. We begin in the backyard and, this April evening, we stop at the apple trees first. The buds have yet to open, but they are fat and dark and swelling with the sap just now reaching them. Each bud the promise of a flower, the invitation to a bee, the shaping of a fruit that will feel my hand twist it from a stem. Chaucer sniffs at the trees' base. Our neighbors have dogs, a set of golden retrievers, and they leave scent messages for each other here. I cup some deer-eaten branches in my palm. Not twenty steps from home, and we're already in the questions that point toward story. Who has come to visit? What have they eaten? Why did they eat from this tree and not the other one? What did they need?

A red-headed bird (later, I will be unable to find it in my field guide) flies past us and lands on the porch. Chaucer and I walk past the ash and maple trees. Even here there are stories. The fall gold ash trees struggle, insects having come to visit last year, while the patmore ash trees nearly leap into the season. Beyond our yard there is a berm and then a county ditch, and there are deer prints in the soft soil there. Chaucer bounds from one tree or tuft of grass to another, loping with the gait of a happy dog. Killdeer try to lure him, dragging a wing in faux injury, then flying away.

Every story has a beginning before our entrance. The grass on this berm is ragged and torn, large sections just dirt without green. And there is a reason for this. Last year the river flooded. Famously. The Red River of the North, which flows through Fargo and Grand Forks, North Dakota, had its second five-hundred-year flood in ten years. Sandbag walls and earthen dikes were built by students and volunteers—people driving here from Tennessee and Maine and Washington State to help—at a speed just a foot faster than the river's rise. Homes were lost, though most were saved. In our backyard, the clay wall rose nearly eight feet higher than the yard it protected. When the flood receded, the wall was removed. The missing grass is the only remainder.

I know this story because I was here. But how many stories, how many small remainders of something huge and deep, do I pass each day without the insight to ask? Where I live was once a Pleistocene sea. Where I live was once the home of dinosaurs. I have a porch on the unsteady earth.

There are clouds to the west, low and gray and stormish, and there will be rain later tonight. More troubling, however, is the rising plume of black smoke to the north. Something is on fire. All I can see at the moment is the effect of some cause on the ground. When I get home I will learn there has been a backyard accident. A young boy is badly burned. A neighbor who came to his rescue is dead.

We turn from sidewalk to bike path and Chaucer's head comes up. This is normally where we meet Angus, a small black terrier on a walk with his owners, a biology professor from the college and his wife. Our routines match nearly enough that we expect each other here. This place is made by the history of our meeting and by the anticipation of its happening again. But Angus is not here today, and Chaucer sniffs the grass to see what news there might be.

This walk is familiar in the best sense of the word, something close to family and relations, something intimate and protective. Another friend works in her backyard garden. Children play at a city park. A spaniel named Bailey chases a ball and runs up to greet Chaucer, tail wagging. Red-winged blackbirds perch in the reeds at the pond while a loon dives and surfaces in the water. A judge turns dinner on a backyard grill while her dog, a dust mop named Bear, feints and charges us.

At the same moment, this walk is fresh ground, terra incognita, evidence of both entropy and genesis in every step. Homes I have seen for years have been lifted from the earth and placed on steel beams—relocation after the floods. The river, still in flood stage though receding, remakes its banks. Storm clouds shape and filter twilight just this one way once. Birdsong arrives unexpected and fresh. Lights inside houses begin to come on, making shapes in the neighborhood that shift and dance. The landing lights of an airplane appear next to Venus. I can feel the arch of my own feet against the earth.

In other words, I have history in this place. But I have never been in this moment.

Chaucer and I turn a corner and see a man walking the same path, walking faster than we are. And when he is close enough, I see he is a man I have known for years, another colleague at the college, a religion scholar, though through a thousand variations I have never seen him on this walk before. He slows his pace so we can say hello and talk for a few steps. I learn he is about to leave, a three-week trip to the Holy Land. He can't wait, he says. And soon enough he regathers his pace, the appeal of departures lifting his feet. Godspeed, we say. Bon voyage.

A row of lilac bushes fronts the home of friends and a Gordon setter named Emma. If dogs have friends, then Emma is Chaucer's very best. But Emma is not out today. For the remaining mile, Chaucer's walk grows slow, and I slow my own walk, too. We are inbound now. What stories there are have been collected and placed alongside the stories of yesterday and the day before, next to the open space for the stories of tomorrow and the days after that. If coming home is a sign of commitment and love, then setting out is a sign of hope. The arc between setting out and coming home is what keeps us alive.

Our lives are grounded by history and science and empathy. Our lives are lofted by how those things meet each unexpected sight. Sometimes the leaving is only to walk my dog. Sometimes the hope is a good bit larger. Tell me a story, the Innkeeper said. Tell me a story.

I have come to believe that my dog understands the idea of a story. Collies are herding dogs. Every molecule in every muscle is tuned to the act of meeting the flock, or collecting the stray, of heading out alone to come back with more. Every day, what he finds is the change from the day before. Someone new has marked the trail. Someone he expects has failed to appear. Deer, rabbits, turkeys and moose have scented this day's chapter. The trees are a different color. The wind carries news from some other part of the territory. The North American Plate has moved a millimeter west.

Heading out is an act of desire. If I want my dog to leap to his feet, all I need to say, softly or not, is "Ready?"

I always ask it as a question. The answer is always an adrenaline yes.

Prairie Sky

River Flying

The Sheyenne River

Imagine winter on the northern prairie. January cold. Deep hard snow. Blizzard one day—winds that can freeze your breath before it leaves your body—bright clear sky the next.

Now imagine a small airplane low in the sky, white wings in a steep bank to the left over the intersection of two frozen rivers. Riparian trees, mostly oak and elm, outline the river course, every brown limb and branch defined against the snow and ice like a fine pencil sketch on a planetary scale. Where the wind has blown the snow away, the rivers shine as if the sun were inside the ice.

Here is a truth, perhaps a secret, about the northern prairie. Winter is the most beautiful season. Beautiful in the way hoarfrost hangs from trees. Beautiful in the way snow can fall so gently you believe, for more than just a moment, you've entered a place both sacred and deep. Beautiful in the way that cold air can kill you fast. Beautiful in the way that sun dogs in the morning can make it seem like three suns ignite the horizon. Beautiful in the hard contrasts of winter light, every shape a crisp edge. Beautiful in the way that clear sky on a midwinter night is so quiet you swear you can hear the radio voices of stars. Beautiful in the way that every story is about staying alive, and beautiful in the way that people smile when they tell them.

Earlier this morning, a full moon shaded from white to yellow and then amber as it set. Yellow last night at rising. Bright crystal white at midnight.

Yellow at setting. At sunrise, the temperature was eighteen degrees below zero. The windchill was minus thirty-eight.

Two thousand feet above the ground, I level the airplane wings. This is where the Sheyenne River meets the Red River of the North, and I want to follow the Sheyenne. Upriver, I think. Always upriver. Upriver is toward what came before us, before here, before now. Upriver is history rushing at us. Downriver is water I've already seen. Not history. Just the past.

I want to match the river turns and meanders, to feel the press of every river bend in my back and chest. There is a love between the airplane and the boat or ship—the captain of one nods to the pilot of the other. Currents and tide are winds and pressure. I want to put this airplane's shadow on the river ice and go exploring.

The whole prairie is frozen. But if you live here, you learn early the lesson that snow and ice can jump and dance. Drifts can build and disappear, sometimes migrate across the landscape. A few inches of new snow can blow into a wall that's taller than a home. The frozen river roils underneath the ice. I want to see the Dakota snowfields that will melt into this river. We already know a disaster is coming. This has been a hard winter. The ground was wet and full last fall when the frosts came, and the snowfall has been consistent, full of water. We already know the rivers will flood. We've been here before: 1997, 2009. Countless other years that did not make the national evening news. Sandbag walls to protect people's homes. Diversions cut into the earth to protect the towns.

This January day, however, I want to see the frozen world. I want to fly in the fat smooth air, to see the prairie at a truer scale, to fill my eyes with the size of this place.

It's almost like ballet. Preflight. Starting. Warm-up. The voices from the control tower—the instructions. Taxiing. The rush down the runway. Airborne. There are names for every move. The run-up. Position and hold. Every move needs to be learned, practiced, made so familiar you feel the patterns in every other thing you do. It's technical, yes. But there is a grace to getting metal and bone into the sky.

This morning at the airport, the automated weather announcement gives a clue about the depth of this season. "Temperature minus two three, dew point minus two eight, altimeter three zero two five. . . . Notice to airmen, Runway One-Three/Three-One closed, Runway Niner/Two-Seven PAPI lights out of service, airport signs are obscured . . ." We've just had that much snow.

"Fargo ground," I say, calling the control tower, "Cessna One Zero Eight Nine Seven is at the north ramp ready to go. Departing to the north, then going to turn and follow the Sheyenne River, please. At or below three thousand."

"Cessna One Zero Eight Nine Seven, Fargo ground," a pleasant female voice comes over the radio. "Taxi to Runway Three-Six at Bravo Three intersection via Charlie at Bravo, maintain at or below three thousand, departure frequency 120.4, squawk 0454."

"Zero four five four," I say, confirming the squawk code.

"Cessna Eight Nine Seven, verify your route of flight, please," she asks.

I can imagine the controllers in the tower. Fargo gets a lot of air traffic, but most airplanes here are in or out. Most flight lessons go to one of four practice areas, defined by space on the ground and altitude in the air, or practice instrument procedures along published routes. What's this guy doing? they wonder.

"I'd like to follow the Sheyenne River," I say. "So a departure to the north, then an immediate turn left, and then south, around to Lake Ashtabula via Kindred."

"Cessna Eight Niner Seven, roger."

My airplane today is a Cessna 172. A small four-seater, high wing with a single prop. It's a good airplane for flying low and slow, for looking at the ground and chasing ideas.

"Fargo ground, FAA Three Eight Nine," a man's voice in the radio now. "I'm at the north Flight School building. I'd like to proceed on foot to the One Eight PAPIs to remove some snow."

"Cessna Three Eight Nine, proceed as requested."

Cessna, I think? The lady in the tower is probably smiling now at her mistake. The poor FAA guy is probably smiling, too. Shovel in hand, he's about to trudge his way to dig out the lights that tell pilots if they are on a proper glideslope toward the runway.

At the runway, the final checks are easy, and the engine sounds smooth. A twin-engine airplane lands and crosses in front of me, its red paint bright against the snow.

"Fargo Tower," I say. "Cessna One Zero Eight Nine Seven is at Bravo Three ready to go."

"Cessna One Zero Eight Niner Seven at Bravo Three, fly runway heading, cleared for takeoff."

"Cleared for takeoff, Eight Nine Seven, thank you," I say.

And then that most wonderful thing. The throttle goes in; the plane moves forward. You steer with your feet, a light hand on the yoke, and when the airspeed indicator gets to about 60, you pull back, just a bit, and the nose tilts up.

Suddenly, you are flying.

Here is another truth. What a pilot sees is a world revealed. The horizon races away as the airplane climbs. Railways, highways, riverbeds, forests and farmland all become part of the same one picture. The next town over, usually just a name on the weather map during the evening news, is right there in front of you, the whole thing, connected to everything else. The silver grain bins at a farmstead, the yellow school bus crawling down a snow-covered neighborhood road, the snapping flags at a shopping center are all part of one window's view. When the airplane and I get to three thousand feet above sea level, which here is two thousand one hundred feet above the ground, I can see what feels like the whole of this day in motion.

"Cessna One Zero Eight Nine Seven," the voice in my headset says, "Fargo departure. Radar contact. Turn left and proceed to the Sheyenne River."

"Do you mind if I go a bit farther north?" I ask. "So I can catch the intersection with the Red?"

"Eight Nine Seven, request approved. Advise when you start your turn to the left, please."

"Will do. Eight Nine Seven."

Oh, I say to myself, what a beautiful day up here. Bright sunshine on the snowfields. Brown trees along the meanderings and oxbows of the Red River stand in stark contrast to the white ice and snow. I can see the Sheyenne in front of me. More trees on the riverbanks. A path leading west and then turning south. Where the two rivers meet, the ice field is a bit wider. It just looks like a field. You would never know there was water moving underneath.

I call departure and let them know I am turning left. Then I turn on a voice recorder to make some notes, and without thinking I also press the airplane's microphone key.

"Hard meanders left and right," I say. "Very pretty in the sunshine where the rivers meet."

"Cessna Eight Nine Seven, roger that," departure says.

Oh, bother, I think, smiling.

The entire prairie is covered in a hard pack of snow. Only the trees give any relief or contrast. Roads are nearly invisible, light gray in the white fields. Railways make a fainter line as well, snow on the berms and dusting the tracks.

The wind is from the north at 14 knots and absolutely smooth. This is the grace of flying in winter air. Airspeed is 115 knots. Altitude is three thousand feet. I bank to the left as the river turns south. Upriver, I think.

———————————————————

Every river is a story.

The Sheyenne is an ancient and meandering river. The loop of one oxbow is often not twenty yards from the end of another, though the water takes a quarter mile to get there. This river was here in the Pleistocene, draining the prairie to Lake Agassiz, the largest inland sea in North America, a sea that covered most of Manitoba and reached into Saskatchewan, Ontario, the Northwest Territories, and Minnesota, larger than the Great Lakes combined. Back then, the Sheyenne would have looked like the Missouri or Mississippi River today. Huge. Glacier-cut valleys in places. Flatland wanderings everywhere else. The river is older than the last ice age. Glacial drift filled the riverbed, and the river works to clean it out. Three hundred and twenty-five miles long, it drains nearly ten thousand square miles. And there is a chance it could drain trouble. Devil's Lake, north and west of here, has no natural outlet and is rising fast, eating homes and farmsteads and roads and railways as it grows. When it overflows the natural banks, it will drain into the smaller Stump Lake and then into the Sheyenne. The Sheyenne joins the Red, which flows north, through Lake Winnipeg and finally into Hudson Bay. Canada does not want Devil's Lake water at all.

In the western distance, I can see some clouds moving in, although the clouds are high. Pinks and blues in the clouds. But no color on the ground. No reds. No greens. No browns. The whole world is one white snowscape. Glistening ice in the fields. Softer white where the snow is deep. Every building has a snowcap on the roof, as does every silo, every farmstead, every home. *Blanket* is exactly the right word.

I can see the West Fargo fairgrounds, but only because I know they're there. The snow erases and covers the way the ground is used.

The holes in the clouds are not the small round holes that let beams of godlight through. They are more like changes of color on a map, where the elevation of the terrain gains or loses altitude.

How much snow is there? How fast is this river moving? These are the important questions in a winter of deep snow.

So far we've had fifty-six inches of snow. The Weather Service says there are only twenty-one inches of snow on the ground today, but over time snow compresses and hardens, settles into every possible space. The water equivalent is nearly four inches. Hundreds of miles in every direction, under at least four inches of standing water. And all of that water wanting to move.

At the Baldhill Dam, 271 upriver miles from north of Fargo where the Sheyenne empties into the Red, the water is flowing at 320 cubic feet per second. Too low to come over the spillway, the water drains from pipes in the bottom of Lake Ashtabula. On this day in 1956, the water was flowing at only 2 cubic feet per second. Before today, the maximum flow on this date was 306 cubic feet per second in 2001. The maximum flow ever, no matter the date, was 6,200 cubic feet per second on April 17, 2009. In other words, the river isn't fast, but it's the fastest it's ever been in the hard freeze of winter.

Yesterday, I called the Army Corps of Engineers, the St. Paul office that oversees the dam, and talked with Richard Schueneman, who is the Corps of Engineers' North Dakota Flood Control Section supervisor. "We're drawing the lake down as far as possible," he told me. "We want to get down to 1,257 by March 1. We're anticipating a lot of water coming in this spring."

I bank to the right, wondering if I can turn as fast as the river. Even with the airplane tilted nearly sixty degrees, back pressure on the yoke to maintain altitude, I cannot match the bend. Some pilots like to get low over wide rivers, settle in as if they were speedboats with wings. It doesn't work if the river is narrow, meandering, folding back toward itself a thousand times. There would be no way to fly the actual course of the river. Too many hard loops and turns, too many bends in the path. Even the slowest airplane, with the steepest angles of turn, would overshoot these banks. If I were at river height, I'd be smashing through the trees.

I am not very far above the river, however. My altitude, measured to sea level, has been the same since I took off. But the land is rising. I am nearly five hundred feet closer to the ground than I was when I made the first turn and announced to the radio world that the frozen river mouth glittered in the daylight. Here, however, there is nothing on the river. There were snowmobile tracks in some places before, but not now. I pass expensive river homes in new neighborhoods, homes too new to know the deep history of how a river behaves, sold perhaps in autumn when the river is low and an empty canoe tied to a tree seems like a promise of forever. But then those homes disappear behind me, and all I see is the snow, the trees, the cornices on bare banks, the shape of finger drifts downwind.

A tree farm appears on the southern bank, ordered rows of small evergreens sticking out of the white.

There are days I wish I knew a lot more than I know. There are days I wish I were a meteorologist, a glaciologist, a historian, an anthropologist, and, yes, even an astronaut. Today I wish I were a geologist. Flying over the river, all I can do is wonder what makes the river find this particular course. What resistance in the soil at one spot is missing or doubled in another? What causes the yielding of erosion here? I wonder if it's all accidental. I wonder if it was cataclysmic—a flood moving through to reorder everything. This happened to the Mississippi at the New Madrid fault. This happened to the Columbia and Clark Fork when the ice dams broke. Even the Yukon used to flow south—the evidence in the rocks of valleys long dry and off-course. The cutoff oxbow lakes and ponds show where the Sheyenne used to be, but how did this river appear? One hundred million years ago, in the Cretaceous, this was all under saltwater. The Western Interior Seaway and the Hudson Seaway joined here. The water was warm, tropical, and shallow. There were sharks and giant clams. There were beasts named Mosasaur and Xiphactinus and Cretoxyrhina. And then the seaways drained. The earth changed. One hundred thousand years ago the ice moved in and stayed. The Laurentide ice sheet covered North America south to the Missouri River. Ten thousand years ago it left, and the meltwater and drainage made Lake Agassiz, the largest inland sea on the planet. I know the Sheyenne is older than the glaciers, but I don't know how.

A red barn in the snow. A row of young pine trees at another farmstead, just struggling, it seems, to make it through this winter, to keep their branches above the snow line, to find another summer to grow.

Snowball earth, I think. Seven hundred and fifteen million years ago. The whole planet frozen and still. But a tremendous pressure building under the ice.

Airspeed 112 knots. Course 198 degrees.

South of the town of Kindred, the trees grow more numerous, the shelter-belts more prominent and thick. Around the river, the line of riparian trees becomes a forest. It would be possible to lose the winter thread of the river in the trees, the snow filling in the low spots, nearly level from field through forest. Over the river and through the woods, I smile, to the next open field of ice.

According to the instruments in the airplane, the outside air temp is minus 1 degree Fahrenheit. A lot warmer up here than it is on the ground. Cold air sinks. Snow and ice reflect the sun back into space. Snow and ice compress and harden.

There are hills here. You almost can't see them because of the snow. Nothing spectacular. Ten feet. Twenty feet, maybe. The Sheyenne National Grasslands. This is where Lake Agassiz ended. This is beachfront property. This is where glaciers left moraines.

South of the town of Leonard, a yellow barn surrounded by snow. The river bends, cuts underneath me, and then cuts back. If you know the grasslands are there, you can imagine what is beneath the snow. But today, just white fields. Smaller, younger trees stick up out of the freeze.

The size of the sky and the size of the earth here, where the land is flat, are gut-stealing at times. South of the town of Sheldon, the river takes a hard turn to the south and the trees thin out again. No marks on the river ice. The day has been growing dimmer, softer, more gray as the weather gets close. A hole in the clouds in the southern distance lets the sunlight through and the prairie beneath it sparkle. The ceiling now is overcast at seventy-five hundred feet. The wind is easy, 020 at 10. Visibility is still ten miles. The temperature on the ground is minus 23 degrees Celsius. Minus 9 degrees Fahrenheit.

Colors are aqua blue, pink, chromium steel, purple, bright piercing white. Not on the ground, however. These are the colors of clouds today. Some of the light is filtered from the sunshine above. Some of the light is reflected from the ice fields below. All of it subtle. All of it mesmerizing.

Trying to keep the river off the left side of the airplane so I can look out my window and down at it, I've given up trying to match the bends in the river to the banks and turns of airplane. I'm looking for something else now, I think, though I'm not sure what. Where the river makes a turn to the west, a red house rises from the snow. A beautiful home. Barn inspired, but clearly a home and not a utility building. A posh home. Frozen in place. Nothing else around it. No outbuildings. No plowed driveway. I have no idea how anyone is getting to or from it. It may be new enough no one lives there.

What I am looking for, it occurs to me, is simply evidence. Evidence of what came before this day. Evidence of what is still on its way.

One hundred and twenty-three years earlier, in 1888, a January morning like this was the morning after what came to be known as the Children's Blizzard. Schoolchildren, having gone to school in light jackets because the air had become unseasonably warm, froze to death on their way home. Montana, the Dakotas, Minnesota, Nebraska, Iowa—the whole of the American prairie. Lethal cold, terrible wind, white-out snow, you couldn't see your hand at the end of your arm. Your eyes froze shut. You literally suffocated on the fine-crystal powder snow. The temperature fell in some places to nearly minus 40 as fast as wind moves across a lake. Somewhere between 250 and 500 people dead in one night because the cold came so hard and so fast.

Only a few years ago, in 1997, a mother and daughter drove off the road in a blizzard and then froze to death in the yard of a farmstead they could see but could not reach.

Only last week, a man froze in his car after he drove off a rural road and into a snowbank. He did not have a telephone. He could not walk to save his life.

The river runs west. Open ground with tremendous drifts where something creates a wind shadow. Nowhere near any school or town, I pass four baseball fields, home plates at the middle of the pie-shaped fields, making it all look like a strange, white four-leaf clover. Evergreens planted just outside the home-run fences look like green dots in the white drifts. The river turns north, and I bank the airplane to follow. Where the county roads are open, no cars dare make the journey.

In truth, today is not a difficult day. By northern standards, the temperature and sky today hardly warrant a moment's thought. People will forget their gloves today and decide not to go back to retrieve them. But the newspaper yesterday gave voice to what we have known for some time. Front page and above the fold, a story began: "A snowier than usual winter and a grim flood outlook expected today from the National Weather Service have spring flood preparations ramping up early this year. Both Fargo and Cass County are ready to issue emergency declarations following today's flood forecast, a move usually made much later in the spring."

This morning, again front page, the reporter continued:

> The chances for another record-breaking flood in Fargo-Moorhead deepened Tuesday. . . . High soil moisture content and excessive snowfall and precipitation in the fall and winter signal the probability of the significant flooding, said Greg Gust, weather service warning coordination meteorologist in Grand Forks. . . . The Red River Basin is poised to receive twice its normal snowfall through the end of the winter, Gust said. To compound the problem, most of the same area received 10 to 12 inches above normal rainfall during the summer and fall, he said. . . . Based on climatic outlooks, this spring is likely to be cooler and spring thaw could come later than the past couple years, Gust said. If the melt comes in April, warmer temperatures can lead to a rapid runoff, which happened in 1997.

It's difficult to look out the window and not see the past, I think. It's difficult to not imagine the future. Only a month ago, on Christmas Eve, the headline was clear. "Forecast: Major Flood Likely."

West of Lisbon, some cattle feed in a corral. The earth is brown and muddy under their feet.

North and west of Lisbon, trees give evidence of a main valley and a network of smaller rifts cutting away to the sides. Looking like hash marks leading down to the water, the trees forest the small ravines.

I've seen this before, I think. Not this particular site. But I've seen this tone, this mood, this emotion in the land. I stare at the river in the new valley, and it comes to me. I am looking at a tombstone rubbing! The strokes of black or gray. The hard white of the paper. If not a rubbing, then a woodcut. There are no subtleties at first. Everything is hard white or hard brown. But then you look, and you realize there is no such thing as a broad stroke. Every white is a thousand shades. Every brown is a thin line amid a million thin lines. A smudge in a tree becomes a squirrel's nest. A spot on the river is a deer finding its way across.

Coming up on Fort Ransom, the valley gets a bit deeper. The river turns north. A couple brown areas come into view, cornfields left standing southeast of Kathryn.

Course: 340 degrees. Airspeed: 110 knots. Altitude: 3,000 feet.

The valley grows wide. And in the valley, the river does not meander. In the Skyhawk, the GPS moving map tells me there are lakes around here. One to my right. One to my left. Looking out my window, I can't find any clue of where they really are.

I approach Valley City, a pretty town even in snow and ice with its famous trestle bridge for the railway. The interstate highway is a clear ribbon on the prairie. Not as clear as the trees or the valley, though. North of the interstate, the railway runs east and west.

A long, dark streak in the snow appears. There is open water north of Valley City! The river is open! Beautiful sight, I say to myself and the recorder. Scattered ice on the river crowds into bends and corners, but the river is open. I have to be close to the dam. Yes, there it is! The end of Lake Ashtabula. I can't tell the lake is there—it looks like just another field at the moment—but the water south of the dam is open, steam rising off the water. I can see the spillway, then two more basins and drops for the water. Then the frozen lake.

I know the water in the river is coming from the bottom of the lake where the water temperature is just one degree above freezing. I know the water takes ten days to get from here to the intersection with the Red. And I know the reason the water is open is because the warmer water is coming out fast for this time of year. But I am happy to see the open water. Potential energy made kinetic, I think. Or just the deep beauty of moving water. Something ancient in all of us.

I turn the airplane east, toward home. In front of me, a forest of pale-white wind turbines turns slowly in the winter air. This has been a very good day. I have seen the past, I think. Which is to say I've seen what's coming our way.

Behind me now, weather's coming in. Snow in the forecast for tonight.

Short-Hop Notebook

Dakota Sky

How different North Dakota felt! I had spent a week flying in the canyons of Idaho—a mountainside off each wing tip, a wild river below—with the thought of engine failure strictly repressed, of course: no use thinking about it where you simply can't afford one! I had flown down into North Dakota through night, a black night, with nothing visible but the beacons along the airway; and again the forced-landing idea had been switched off—there are lots of badlands on that route. Toward morning, not to get too low on gas, I had sat down on an Auxiliary Field to wait for daylight. It was deserted. (Those fields are not built to serve a town, but to serve the airway—they sit there, every hundred miles or so, their boundaries outlined by lights, just in case.) Parked there under the beacon tower, I had fallen asleep right in the airplane.

I woke up and it was daylight. I started her up, and took off. Still dull in mind, I cleared the fence. There it was: Landings unlimited. You cleared the fence and you had cleared everything. As far as the eye could see, big fields—flat as a table and bigger than airports. And smoothly cultivated: where farm machinery can roll, airplane tire can also roll. It was fall, and most of them were stubble. The nice, combed-looking stubble of machine-sown wheat: a guaranteed surface, along with unlimited room.

"This," I thought, "is 100 percent O.K. This is the rose without the thorn; this is the meal that is all dessert; this goes in easy." In fact, I swear I had a strong sensation as if I were a little boy again and had just been handed a dish of whipped cream with chocolate.

"I think I'll just roll my wheels on that one." I had only flown a minute, but why not? "I'll fly straight for exactly three minutes, and then close my throttle." Nothing to it—just glide straight ahead. I thought it would be fun to roll up to a fence and jump it and sit right down again, so I did. Why not? "I think I'll spiral up to 1,000 feet and cut my ignition and stop my prop." Done.

Now, I don't claim it is a red-hot and brand-new idea that North Dakota is different from New England. I tell it to show you how a pilot reacts to the country: he does react; he can't help it. And not as a tourist; he is not ever "just looking." He has business with the country, and the country with him.

—Wolfgang Langewiesche, author of *Stick and Rudder,*
from his essay "American Air" in the book *A Flier's World*

A Wall of Old Trees

"This looks promising," Gerry says.

I put the airplane, a little Cessna 172, tail number One Two Whiskey, into a hard right turn, following his hand pointing out the window, and lower the nose toward the earth of the Red River Valley. For just a moment, we are both a bit lighter in our seats. I am aiming for a stand of trees, five or six rows deep, what looks like oak and evergreens bordering a gravel county road. The airspeed indicator climbs past 110 knots.

"You just can't tell, can you?" he asks.

One thousand feet above the prairie, I pull back on the yoke, and we pass another row of trees as I bank the airplane to the left, heading a bit more south. Gerry scans the prairie landscape to the horizon. All I see is farmland below us, divided into neat and orderly sections. A week or so past harvest, the land looks dry and empty. Desert, almost. Flatland. A few rows of trees protect farmsteads, but the overall image is almost frighteningly open and exposed.

Some distance in front of us, the North Dakota sand hills rise to break the grid. The southern end of Pleistocene glacial Lake Agassiz. The Sheyenne National Grasslands now. The Sheyenne River. Riparian ecosystems. Riverbank forests. South of the town of Leonard, the trees get thick, and my hopes begin to rise until Gerry says, "You know, most of this was just recently taken out of production. CRP lands. It's all very young."

Damn, I think.

Gerry and I are on a mission. We are looking for a wall. A huge wall. An old wall. A wall big enough to stop the wind.

Imagine what must have been a very strange conversation.

"Build a wall," someone said.

The room went silent.

"They'll just go around it" came the practical reply.

It could have been in the eighth century BCE. It could have been much later, somewhere between 403 and 331 BCE. It could have been during the Spring and Autumn period. It was certainly somewhere in the seven states that now make up China.

"Then build a really big wall," the first person said. "Not tall," he continued, "just really, really long. Connect what we already have." He might have stood in the middle of the room, arms outstretched, a smile on his face.

Perhaps there was silence, or laughter, or outrageous argument. Perhaps the guy was tossed out of the room and into the muck of the street. But at least one other person sat back in his chair, his mind already whirring with the math.

We climb. One thousand five hundred feet above the North Dakota prairie, Gerry and I are looking for a wall. Huge, I tell him. Magnificent and enormous, I say. It was supposed to be a hundred miles wide, stretching all the way from Canada to Mexico. Not a hundred miles thick, but an interlaced system of rows of trees evenly spaced that would stop nothing less than the wind itself. Dust Bowl days. The whole of the farmland Midwest in drought, the soil turned and baked, then lifted by the wind and carried off in great walls of silt and suffering.

The evidence should be everywhere. When a story gets big enough, it leaves its marks on the earth. Glaciers dig out the Great Lakes and fill in the Manson Crater, leave marks on Dakota fields. Long Island is a terminal moraine. Ancient riverbed rocks betray the old course of the Yukon River, south to the Pacific Ocean. A rock from heaven makes Lake Manicouagan. Old trails in the desert and forest and grasslands still nearly glow in evening light. Or maybe it's the other way around—marks on the earth are the syllables of words of stories, dreamtime songlines for all of us. It doesn't matter. Sometimes you hear a story and you want to touch the earth. Sometimes you touch the earth and want to hear a story.

I don't remember when I first heard this story. A living wall right down the middle. A wall to stop the wind. The evidence should be everywhere. But I know from the ground I will never see the whole hope. What I need is altitude.

"You want to go flying?" I asked. "We should be able to see it everywhere."

We can't find any trace at all.

Clear late-September sky. Bright sun. Temperatures in the sixties. A steady wind from the north at 20 knots, forecast to increase as the day goes on. The airplane lifts easily off the runway, and we turn left, west, and then left again, southwest, leveling off at two thousand five hundred feet above sea level, only one thousand five hundred feet above the ground. A perfect altitude for scanning the land.

This is where the maps show the wall, and the story, should be. The dragging and scouring of glacial ice. The shape of old Lake Agassiz. The flooding at Devil's Lake. We should be able to find this wall. We fly over the grasslands, beautiful in late-summer color, through sunlight reflecting off river water and silo tops.

West of the airport, North Dakota seems as ordered and measured as a chess board. Every mile a section road running north and south. Every mile a section road running east and west. A farmstead on nearly every section. The grains and beans have been harvested. Sugar beets just beginning to be lifted.

"Look at those fields, all that brown," he says. "Those must have all been beans."

Gerry is a field biologist, a specialist in streams and river ecosystems. Long-time chair of his department at the college and deeply, creatively curious, it would be difficult to find anyone who knows the prairie better.

"The perspective up here is *wonderful*," he says.

We pass West Fargo and the interstate highway. There are very few trees. Some small stands protect the north and west sides of homes. A grove of shade trees offers comfort at a small and isolated cemetery.

We pass the town of Davenport and head southwest toward Leonard. In front of us the land changes completely. Level fields change into the sand hills. Open cropland becomes forest. This is a continental divide. North of the hills, water flows to the Red River and then to Lake Winnipeg, eventually to Hudson Bay, and then the North Atlantic. South of the hills, water flows to the Missouri River, then the Mississippi, then the Gulf of Mexico.

"This looks promising," Gerry says.

Fast forward to AD 122.

Somewhere in Britain, or perhaps Rome, important people are talking about their border problems. The Scots just keep coming.

"Build a wall," someone suggests.

"They'll just go around it" is the practical reply.

"Then build a really big wall," the first person says. "Not tall," he continues, "just really, really long. We can name it after Emperor Hadrian."

There is silence, or laughter, or outrageous argument. Perhaps the guy is tossed out of the room and into the muck of the street.

And then fast-forward another 1,788 years. The French, after World War I, look at Maginot and the continuing threat of the German army.

"We could build a wall," someone said. "All the way from Switzerland to Luxembourg."

"They'll just go around it" was the practical reply.

And of course they did.

Plains forestry became front-page news in the summer of 1934 when the Department of Agriculture and Forest Service announced to the nation the enormous Shelterbelt Project. The "New York Times" and "Herald-Tribune" explained to a puzzled public that President Franklin Roosevelt had issued an executive order allocating $15 million in drought relief funds for a tree-planting project on the Great Plains. And that was only the beginning. Over the next ten years, Roosevelt would request $75 million for the project, which was a huge sum of money in 1930s America. The project was equally large. The plan called for constructing a one hundred mile wide zone of shelterbelts, spread one mile apart, and running continuously from the Canadian border to the Texas Panhandle. The 1200-mile long parallel forests would be America's Great Wall, holding back the dust, drought, and despair of the Dust Bowl.

Although public reaction was a mixture of ridicule, adulation, and sheer disbelief, the plan was everything that some foresters had long dreamed of for the Plains. They believed that the Timber Culture Act had failed, not because trees had failed, but because farmers had lacked the necessary knowledge and skills. Likewise, the reserve movement had been a good, but under-funded, idea in need of more systematic planning. Plans for cooperative tree distribution were by their very nature, too limited and too prone to some of the same failures as the Timber Culture Act. Foresters hoped that the Shelterbelt Project would correct previous errors by bringing the full scientific, budgetary, and bureaucratic might of the federal government to bear on the problem.

—Joel Orth, *The Conservation Landscape:*
Trees and Nature on the Great Plains

The story is apocryphal.

March 21, 1935. Hugh Hammond Bennett, *Big Hugh,* a man from North Carolina extraordinarily interested in soil conservation, the man who would eventually found and lead the Soil Conservation Service, is testifying at a Senate hearing. Too many years of bad practices, he says. Too many years of "black blizzards." The country needs to get its farming to match its farms and its weather. But he might as well be wearing a sandwich board reading, "Repent! The End Is Near!" The senators, according to the story, could not be more uninterested and bored.

The problem is obvious. The wind is picking up the prairie soil and taking it away. North Dakota dirt fills the windowsills and gutters of Pittsburgh and

Roanoke. South Dakota, Nebraska, Kansas, Oklahoma, and Texas recoat the Appalachians and Alleghenies. The Dust Bowl is real. Too much dirt has been turned over and loosened for planting. There isn't enough rain to keep it all in place. Drought is here. Famine is on its way. To say the rain follows the plow is a wonderful slogan. Too bad it isn't true.

Bennett knows a storm is coming. His speech lingers. His weather data are excellent. Soon, he thinks. He adds a few details. The Senate windows are open. Glasses of water are set out. And then it hits. Rolling in from the prairie and over the mountains, a cloud of yellow dust covers the Capitol, billows through the open windows, and collects on glasses turning to mud.

"This, gentlemen, is exactly what I'm talking about!" he cries.

His point is taken.

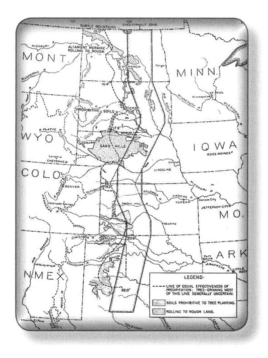

Build a wall to keep something out, they said. Build a wall to stop the invasion. Five thousand five hundred miles for the Great Wall of China. Seventy-three miles from one end to the other for Hadrian. Yes, there is something that doesn't love a wall, but that's never stopped us from trying. Maginot Line, Berlin Wall, Israel-Palestine Wall, the border fence between the United

States and Mexico. The Greenbelt in Niamey. The Green Dam in Algeria. The Greenbelt in Nouakchott. The levees to keep the water out of New Orleans, the dikes to keep Amsterdam dry. Sandbag walls in Fargo and Moorhead. Castle walls fronted by moats. Walls around cities with names like Kowloon, Rhodes, Lucca, and Jericho.

Joel Orth is an assistant professor of history at California Polytechnic University in San Luis Obispo. The view outside his office is an ally of jumbled Australian orange berry and iron-bark gum trees. Tree squirrels sometimes run the branches. He is also the author of a PhD dissertation titled "The Conservation Landscape: Trees and Nature on the Great Plains." Chase any idea and soon enough a name gets repeated. I still cannot find any good map, so I send him an e-mail.

"Hi Joel," I write. "I'm holding your fine article on the Shelterbelt project—I believe it was in a summer issue of *Agricultural History*—and I have a question. Do you have any more detailed maps or locations where these shelterbelts were planted?"

The answer comes from Belgrade, Serbia.

> *Hi Scott,*
> *I'm very out of the office so I can't give you some of the specifics you might like, but it's such a delightful project that I couldn't help but reply quickly.*
> *The Soil Conservation Service (now Natural Resource Conservation Service) did some aerial surveys in the 70s. You can probably find the blurbs about these in the SCS magazine of that era. They may also still be able to put you in touch with the actual people or results of those surveys. The findings in a nutshell were that A) aerial surveys worked, and B) the shelterbelts were getting cut down rapidly to make room for center-pivot irrigation. This was also the big era of changed agricultural policy: from holding back production to hold up prices to price supports to encourage increased production. The best source of records for the project are at the Regional National Archives in Kansas City.*
> *Joel*

Aerial surveys, yes. Marking which shelterbelts came from the thirties? No. Phone calls to Kansas City as well as College Park? Very nice people. No joy.

Gerry points at some trees back toward the east, and the airplane turns to chase. There is a wind-speed indicator on the panel, and I notice the wind is climbing. Twenty-five knots now, straight out of the north. The airplane points slightly windward of our goal to counteract the push of the breeze. Someone on the ground would say we were flying slightly sideways.

Gerry is in charge of the camera, and he takes a picture, a stand of trees, three or four rows deep, deciduous trees in full fall color making a right angle around the north and west sides of a farmstead. Then another picture of another farmstead with the same arrangement.

"Look at this one," Gerry says. He points to a stand, six or more rows deep, set against a county road. A farmstead sits on the other side of the road, protected by the trees, but the whole thing just looks like the trees came first.

"You think?" Gerry asks.

There is no way to tell.

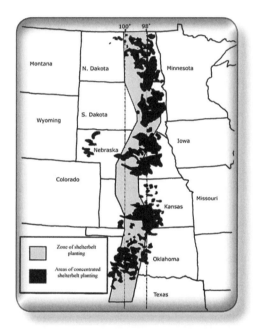

I admit I just don't buy it.

When you take an airplane off the ground, it's not so much that the cars and homes and fields get smaller as much as the planet gets huge. The horizon races away faster than you climb. Just this short leap above the prairie, and I cannot believe a tree, any tree, any hundreds of miles of millions of trees would do any good. The atmosphere is a thin layer on our planet, but the globe is big.

I think I know the idea. Shelterbelt to stop the wind. A row of trees that acts just like a snow fence—deflect the wind up, and you create a low-pressure area behind the fence where the snow will gather and drift. The goal is not so much to stop the wind as it is to *empty* the wind. Better yet, the idea is to stop the wind from picking up the soil in the first place. But one thousand five hundred feet above the prairie, every tree and every shelterbelt seem trivial and small. The cottonwoods and burr oaks and poplars and evergreens cannot make any difference at all, I think. The air, even this low, is fat and lumbering and an impossible force to stop.

This is the prairie. Hell, this is North Dakota. This is the place where cars wiggle when they drive through an underpass because suddenly the crosswind stops and drivers can actually drive straight until the other side when they have to steer into the breeze again. Say something like "gentle prairie breeze" in conversation, and people here will laugh at the joke. On the prairie, the press of the wind against your face is as familiar as breathing and as intimate as a kiss or a slap. It is *always* there. East of the Rocky Mountains, the wind is the huge breath of the planet's breathing. If it stops, people get edgy and strangely worried. It only stops when a bigger wind is on the way.

If you are standing on the ground, a tree is tall and firm and strong. From the air, it's a thin twig of hope at best.

I call a friend of mine, Paul Seifert, a physics professor, to make sure I have the process right. And soon, a beer in his hand and a beer in mine at Atomic Coffee, we are looking at math problems.

"Here are the equations needed for projectile motion on the earth," he says. He points at the first one. "This is a basic kinematic equation." He's written a dozen formulas. He turns the paper toward me and then, seeing my face, pauses.

"Okay, how much of this don't you understand?" he asks.

"I got the equal sign down pretty well," I say.

"Okay," he continues, "look at this." He points at the first equation again.

$$h = \frac{1}{2}gt^2$$

"H," he says, "is the height in the vertical direction, assuming the ground is at $h = 0$; g is the acceleration due to gravity, 9.8 ms^{-2}; and t is the time of flight. It is assumed that the particle starts with no initial velocity in the vertical direction. This can be solved for time, to give

$$t = \sqrt{\frac{2h}{g}}$$

"This time will determine how long the particle will stay in the air based on gravity pulling down on it. The distance in the horizontal direction that it will travel during this time is given by

$$d = v_x t$$

"where d is the vertical distance, and v_x is the horizontal velocity or wind speed. Substituting equation two into equation three gives

$$d = \sqrt{\frac{hv_x^2}{4.9}}$$

"Assuming the tree is 30 feet, 9.1 meters, high, and wind speed is 30 mph, 13.4 m/s, the wind shadow will be 18.6 meters, or about 61 feet. Not very far at all."

It seems like a good idea, so I nod my head.

I e-mail some of Gerry's pictures to Joel Orth. He writes:

I'd have a hard time saying about 005. It certainly might be. It's wide with varied species and planted along a roadway with a wide offset (allowing snow to drift without covering the road). The thing that makes me uncertain is the tall row of cotton woods (looks like anyway) on the top seems to be on the outside of the belt rather than at the center. Ideally, these were in the middle rows with progressively shorter species to each side. That might mean the belt was "narrowed" or it might just be a different design. It also appears that there are shrubs planted along either side as sort of an understory planting, another characteristic of especially the earlier SB plantings.

The Soil Conservation Service also started planting belts in the 30s and continued to do so right up to today. I haven't seen many recent plantings in the central plains, but the few I have seen have all been conifers planted in a staggered 2-3 rows. I think they may have planted wider more varied belts in the Northern Plains for longer though . . . but going on the belts I've seen pictured in Soil Conservation, I would say these were typically only 1 or maybe 3 species. All of which makes me *think* 005 is probably an SB or early SCS shelterbelt.

The 0015 looks more like a woodlot. I suppose it might have once been a shelterbelt that was cut off, but I doubt it by the arrangement of the trees. The rows are uneven, and I can't see much in the way of a "hipped roof" design (lowest at sides to tallest in the middle), of course given the age, that isn't a sure sign. The other "off" thing about 0015 is its distance to the roadway. Too close. Maybe the road, and even house were put in later though. . . . There were a variety of programs (Clarke McNary, SCS) that helped farmers put in windbreaks like this. Some even pre-date the SB. My guess would be 0015 was one of these.

Nice pictures. I guess the hard part is going to be figuring out which is which.

Imagine either the hope or the hubris.

At its peak they contemplated literally dividing the United States in half with evenly spaced shelterbelts, running like unbroken corn rows from the Canadian border to the Gulf of Mexico. This grand reorganization would tame nature and stabilize the economy and society.

—Joel Orth, *The Conservation Landscape*

Paul and I stare at his equations.

"Paul," I say, "it still seems to me that no matter how many rows, the carrying capacity of the atmosphere has to be larger than what a row of trees can stop. This seems to me like a tremendously romantic idea that has no hope of succeeding."

"But," he says, "you know—look at that map you sent me. The goal here isn't to keep the wind from reaching the east side of the United States. The goal is to keep the soil in place. This is the strip that's more susceptible to drought and, back then, poor farming practices."

"As a physicist, you're going to look at this idea and this map, and you're going to say this is going to work?" I ask.

Paul hesitates. "It will keep the soil in place anywhere there are trees," he says. "Once the shelterbelts end over here in Missouri and Iowa, the wind is going to pick up, but there won't be any Oklahoma or Kansas soil in it. Once that soil gets into the air, and gets up into the air, it's gone. It's going to fall on the East Coast or farther out to sea. And over here," he says, pointing at Missouri, "you have different types of climates, you have woods, you have hills, you have all sorts of things that prevent the soil blowing away."

It is beginning to make sense.

"Look at this," Paul says. He pulls out an article he's found about snow fences. "Now this is cool because it's scaled to tree height." The graphic shows solid fences, slatted fences, tree rows with and without shrubs in front. "This is basically how much snow, or dirt, is going to pile up behind the fence. It's going to create a pile of snow that extends horizontally thirty-five times its own height. So if our fence, think tree rows, was thirty feet high, the snow piles up for a bit more than one thousand feet. And it will back up *in front* of the fence minus ten times the height, or about three hundred feet."

"That still leaves four-fifths of a mile for the wind to get new soil," I say.

"Yes, it does, doesn't it?"

In the back of my head, I remember something about the mechanics of wind blowing over water, and how something called a long fetch length can make for tremendous waves, and I have a sudden feeling that this math would apply here too. But it's clear the formulas don't all agree, and we get caught up trying to solve the math problems with the calculators in our cell phones.

"So," I say, finally. "It's 1934 and you are the chief scientist in the United States. Are you going to approve this project?"

Paul pauses, and smiles.

"Yes," he says. "I think I would."

Gerry and I turn the airplane back toward the south and the Sheyenne National Grasslands. The Sheyenne River meanders in front of us, and for a moment I consider dropping down to buzz the trees and water course. Just a moment to play, to bank the wings and climb and dive. The trees are thick and everywhere. South of the river, the treelines multiply and cut the sections into chess squares and frames. But the wind-speed indicator bumps up toward 30 knots, and I am a bit concerned. With the wind at that speed, coming dead out of the north, I will be able to nearly hover this airplane into a feather-light landing. But if the direction shifts a bit, I'll have a crosswind landing that may exceed my comfort and talent. It might be time to turn toward home.

"Gerry," I say, pointing at the wind speed, "there's no dust in the air."

"Agriculture," he says, "has changed a lot."

I point the front of the airplane at the rising earth. No longer the ancient lakebed flat of home, the terrain around the river and beyond it rises and folds and twists. It's all very pretty. The harvested fields, all brown, set off the greens and golds of the woods.

"Is that the Agassiz shoreline?" I ask.

"No," he says. "The grasslands are a river delta. The prehistoric Sheyenne used to be a lot bigger. You've seen the valley at Valley City? This little river didn't carve that. The prehistoric Sheyenne ran through there, then south a bit, before turning east to empty into Lake Agassiz. It used to be *a lot* bigger. This is where it emptied."

I am amazed. We climb five hundred feet for a better view, and there it is, a river delta I've never seen in landscape I've traveled for decades. One more story to add to knowing where you are. Huge, I think. Magnificent and enormous.

I want to linger, but the wind is pushing hard against this little airplane and good judgment says it's time to land. We turn the airplane north, and soon there are hardly any trees at all. No wall. Nothing that says this was once the site of disaster and then the hope to defeat it. No mark on the ground says this is the site of something large. Either the wall didn't work, or the desire grew weak. Maybe it started to rain enough to keep the dirt in place. Maybe we just learned where and when and how to turn the soil. It's been nearly eighty years. Maybe the trees just got old and died, their wood a comfort in some bonfire or fireplace. Build a wall, someone said. We've been doing it forever. They are temporary at best.

One thing is constant and sure, however. I listen as the men and women in the Fargo control tower give wind speed and direction to every landing airplane. And I know that every pilot pays attention. You can push your airplane against the wind, but only to a compromise or a standstill. There is no such thing as winning. A draw is the best of all possible worlds.

Short-Hop Notebook

Math Class

There is something beautiful about a formula. It doesn't matter if the formula is on our E6B, the inner workings of a G1000, or in the head of Stephen Hawking; there is a clarity in math about the way the universe works that is both elegant and profound. Sometimes it's simply fun.

Perhaps not strangely, mathematics can answer a more poetic question. "How far away *is* the horizon? How much earth can I see?"

The math is pretty simple. D = 112.88 km $\sqrt{}$ (h). Or, distance equals 112.88 kilometers times the square root of the height of the observer, expressed in kilometers.

If 1,000 feet equals 0.3048 kilometers, and the square root of 0.3048 is approximately 0.552, then distance = 112.88 times 0.552, or distance = 62.309 kilometers. 62.309 kilometers = 204425.8530 feet. Or, to put it simply, if you're 1,000 ft AGL (above ground level), the horizon is 38.71 miles away.

2,000 ft AGL = a horizon at 54.76 miles.

4,000 ft AGL = a horizon at 77.44 miles.

8,000 ft AGL = a horizon at 109.517 miles.

But what is the total landscape in view? Pi times the radius squared is the area of a circle. If, at 2,000 ft AGL, the radius is 54.76 miles, then the total area of the circle around me is 9,415.78 square miles. On a clear day, if I am 4,000 ft AGL, a simple turn around a point will bring 18,830.43 square miles into view.

Clearly, this information is useless for flying.

It's just the reason we fly.

River Flying

The Red River

Thursday

THE FLOOD WARNING CONTINUES FOR THE RED RIVER AT FAR-GO. * AT 9:15 PM THURSDAY THE STAGE WAS 36.9 FEET. * MAJOR FLOODING IS OCCURRING AND FOR THE NEXT 7 DAYS . . . MA-JOR FLOODING IS FORECAST. * MAJOR FLOOD STAGE IS 30.0 FEET. * FORECAST . . . THE RIVER WILL CONTINUE RISING TO BETWEEN 39.0 AND 40.0 FEET BY SUNDAY APRIL 10TH. * THE WILD RICE RIVER NEAR ABERCROMBIE AND THE RED RIVER AT ENLOE HAVE SHOWN DECREASING FLOWS . . . WHICH SUGGESTS THAT THE PRIMARY RISE IS NOW ENTERING THE FARGO AREA. THE CURRENT RATE OF MOVEMENT SUGGESTS THAT THE PRIMARY CREST SHOULD REACH FARGO ON SUNDAY . . . AND POSSIBLY AHEAD OF THE RUN-OFF FROM ANY SIGNIFICANT PRECIPITATION THAT COULD OC-CUR FROM LATE SATURDAY INTO SUNDAY. THIS MEANS THAT IF ANY SIGNIFICANT PRECIPITATION DOES OCCUR AT THE TIME OF THE CREST . . . IT WILL LIKELY MAINTAIN HIGH WATER LEVELS FOR A LONGER PERIOD OF TIME. * IMPACT STATEMENT—AT 40.0 FEET . . . IN FARGO . . . TOP OF THE ISLAND PARK DIKE. IN MOORHEAD . . . RED RIVER IS LAPPING AT THE BASE OF THE HERITAGE HJEM-KOMST INTERPRETIVE CENTER.

—The Weather Channel Alert/National Weather Service

Friday

It's always three syllables.

Oh my God.

Je-sus Christ.

What the hell.

The list could go on. Ho-ly Cow. Look at that. A trinity of breath in the face of doom.

"Fargo ground," I say, "Cessna Six Zero Six Five Mike is at the north ramp, ready to go. Information X-Ray. I'd like to depart to the south and do some river photography, at or below two thousand five hundred feet."

"Cessna Six Zero Six Five Mike," comes the reply, "Fargo ground. Runway One-Eight at the Charlie intersection, taxi via Charlie, maintain at or below two thousand five hundred. Squawk zero four five one."

High noon at the Fargo Jet Center, and my friend Jonathan sits in the right seat, camera at the ready. We are going up to see the river today. The Red River of the North. Just to look, to get a glimpse of the size of the thing. We've had deep, hard snow this past winter, and the snow is melting fast. It's a beautiful spring day. Warm air. Gentle breeze. If it wasn't for the river, you'd think this is exactly what spring should be. But there is this river. Once again, the flood has come.

"Zero four five one," I say.

Jon and I have lived here long enough to have a history, a physical history, with floods: 1997, 2009, 2010. We have a memory in our backs and shoulders from throwing sandbags in ice storms and hail, high-speed emergency help to save the homes of people we rarely knew beyond the simple, profound fact they were our neighbors.

In a sandbag line, or straddling the wall itself, a fast-rising river is both intimate and a mystery. You can feel it against your ankle and thigh. You can feel the want of the water, the way it wants to tear down every sandbag wall and earthen dike. But you can only imagine how large it is. There is an ominous, minor-key chord playing somewhere in the distance, you think. But you cannot tell how far away.

Jon and I have traveled a lot together—London, Delhi, Hong Kong, Christchurch—but this is the first time he's flown with me as the pilot.

"Do you want to steer?" I ask as we begin to taxi.

"Nope," he says. His seat is pushed all the way back so he can use more of the window for pictures and video and his feet cannot reach the rudder pedals.

Air traffic control clears several other airplanes for takeoffs, landings, taxiing to and from the parking areas. Jon hears it all in his headset.

"Do you understand anything they're saying?" I ask.

"Not really," he says. And then a moment later, "Do we have parachutes?"

I know he's teasing me.

"No," I say. "But there *is* an airbag in front of you."

At the runway we wait for a twin engine to take off in front of us.

"Does the wind give you any problem at takeoff?" Jon asks.

"Not really," I say. I can't tell if he's nervous or simply curious.

We're cleared for takeoff, and I push the throttle forward. "Away we go!" I say. The airplane accelerates easily, and we're soon off the ground, climbing and heading south. I look over at Jon, who is looking down at the ground.

"Think I know how to land this thing?" I ask.

He pauses for a moment.

"No clue," he says.

And then it starts. We are only a couple hundred feet off the ground, and the river takes over everything. It's impossible to look anywhere else.

"Look at that!" I say. We've turned slightly left to head down the east side of the Red River, and the airplane is climbing over downtown Fargo. "Look at all that water, the standing water, straight ahead!"

In the distance, past town, acres and acres, whole sections of land, one after the other have gone underwater.

"A lot off to the right, too," Jon says.

It's like one of these scenes in a science fiction movie or television show where you open a door you know well—the door to your home or your bedroom or your office—and what's on the other side has changed. Just below us, the river is three or four times its normal width. We can see the normal river channel, the trees lining each bend and curve. But the trees look like shrubs planted in the water. The camera starts clicking.

The Red River of the North is not an easy river. Five hundred and fifty miles, from the joining of the Bois de Sioux and the Otter Tail Rivers in Breckenridge, Minnesota, past Fargo and Moorhead, past Grand Forks, past Winnipeg, past a hundred smaller towns and a thousand farms, the river drains 48,490 square miles of prairie. It gathers the waters of the Sheyenne, the Wild Rice, the Buffalo, the Pembina, Snake, and Assiniboine. It gathers the waters of eastern North Dakota and western Minnesota. It is the border between the two states. It was a major trade route for the Hudson Bay Company. Legend has medieval Vikings paddling along. The Sioux and the Cree know it well.

Unlike nearly every other river in the country, the Red River flows north. In springtime, the headwaters thaw long before the downstream ice is clear.

The Red is a source for drinking water. The damn thing has run dry. It's also become famous for floods, five-hundred-year floods, which means floods so bad they should happen, on average, only every five hundred years. We've had three of them since I moved to town. In 1997 the flood in Grand Forks was so bad it overran the whole of downtown, which then caught on fire. Fire trucks could not battle the flames because the water was too high for them to get close. In Winnipeg, where the Assiniboine, which itself is 660 miles long and drains more than 70,000 square miles of Manitoba and Saskatchewan, meets the Red, the city has built a marina and shopping area, coffee shops and wine bars. I've been there only twice, I tell Jonathan. Both times the docks were under water.

It's one thing to see a swollen river from the ground, I think, the size of the thing hidden by each bend in the stream. It's another thing to see it from the air. Every bank spilled over. Every oxbow a lake. The ground view brings determination. The aerial view brings humility.

"The overland flooding here is just incredible," I say. "Look at this!"

Jon frames a shot and takes the picture. Frames and shoots. Frames and shoots again. There's really nothing to say. Oh my God.

Every river is a deep river, I think. It really doesn't matter if the river is a stream, a creek, a tributary. We are bound to moving water. There is something *moral* about a river. Not judgmental. Simply a statement of the planet's desire. It would not be far off base, or too sentimental, to say the earth speaks in volcanoes and thunderstorms and tsunamis. It would not be too far afield to say the boreal forest is an expression we should work harder to hear. So it would not be completely odd to say the earth gives itself voice in rivers. It would be wrong, completely wrong, to say a flood is an act for or against anything human. The water doesn't care about us at all. On the other hand, we should be listening intently to what the flood might be saying about the temper of our host.

Jon and I pass the interstate highway, heading south while Jon switches to video mode. Two city parks are completely under water. A peninsula that used to be filled with posh homes has disappeared, the homes bought out by the city after the last flood. The campus of a summer theater and performing arts school has become an archipelago of circular islands, river on one side, flooded farmland on the other.

"This is so sad," Jon says. "Look at all that."

Air traffic control warns me about other airplanes nearby. We are not the only ones flying the flood. The director of FEMA is getting a look. Insurance agents and reporters are getting a look. We pass farmsteads, the barns deep in the stream. And we pass homes surrounded by ring dikes of sandbags and hope. The convent road south of town is impassable.

"There's quite a few going under here," Jon says. He frames and shoots.

"Look over here," I say.

Another pilot makes a radio call. Two bald eagles, he says, just flew past him, heading south.

"Hear that?" I ask Jon.

"What?"

"Two bald eagles heading down the pike, just about our altitude."

"Do you see them?"

"No, they're behind us."

We both stare out the window, reduced to the simplest expressions.

"Look at that," I say. "That's just astounding."

Of course, there is really nothing to say. Every home, every farmstead, has its own story. Every loss is hard. Fifteen hundred feet off the ground, however, what you see is the size of a changing season. It's tremendously beautiful. It's deeply terrifying.

In theory, or in the long view, floods are supposed to be good. They replenish the soils and make farmland richer, more productive. In the short view, they sweep away homes. Two hunters have already died in this one when their boat overturned.

There are old rivers here: the Red, the Sheyenne, the Buffalo, the Wild Rice. But there are new rivers too, wide and shallow, cutting depths in farmland as the melted snowpack tries to move.

"I've done this before," Jon says.

"You have?"

"It was 1975, I think," he says. "My brother—he's four years older than me—he was up here to hoe sugar beets. Twenty, maybe thirty miles north of Moorhead. We have cousins who live up there. We would hear stories from him that he couldn't get out to hoe because it was so wet. We started hearing that it was rainfall—it was June when they were doing this—and I have an uncle who has a plane. So he took us up. We were flying over the farmsteads north of town."

"Do you remember what you saw?" I ask.

"Just water. Water everywhere. It was all over the fields. You could only make out by the treelines where the rivers were. Just water from farmstead to farmstead. I don't remember throwing sandbags, though. It just came too quick. Summer floods."

We turn toward home. Flying up the west side of the river, we see it all again. This is flatland prairie. The Red River is a summertime fiction. This is the bottom of ancient Lake Agassiz.

Two birds, hawk-like, maybe the bald eagles, fly below us. Then the control tower clears us to land. We fly over a bend in the Sheyenne River, swollen and overflowing, as it turns north toward Fargo.

"And it came to pass," I say, "after seven days, that the waters of the flood were upon the earth."

Jon looks at me. "That might be overdoing it," he says.

"And the rain was upon the earth forty days and forty nights."

"Snow," he says. "Not rain."

"And the flood was forty days upon the earth; and the waters increased, and bare up the ark, and it was lift up above the earth."

Jonathan stares at me. "You looked that up just for this flight, didn't you?"

"Yup."

Saturday

The rain begins in the evening.

Sunday

. . . THE FLOOD WARNING FOR RAIN REMAINS IN EFFECT UNTIL 100 PM CDT WEDNESDAY FOR WESTERN BECKER AND CLAY COUNTIES IN NORTHWEST MINNESOTA . . . AND WESTERN OTTER TAIL . . . GRANT AND WILKIN COUNTIES IN WEST CENTRAL MINNESOTA . . . AND CASS . . . BARNES . . . SARGENT . . . RICHLAND AND RANSOM COUNTIES IN SOUTHEAST NORTH DAKOTA . . .

AT 628 PM CDT . . . WIDESPREAD . . . AND IN SOME AREAS UNPRECEDENTED . . . OVERLAND FLOODING CONTINUED ACROSS THE AREA. THIS FLOODING WILL CONTINUE FOR THE FORESEEABLE FUTURE. UP TO ONE QUARTER OF AN INCH OF RAIN COULD FALL THROUGH THIS EVENING . . . WHICH COULD MAKE THE FLOODING SITUATION EVEN MORE DIRE IN SOME AREAS.

SEVERE OVERLAND FLOODING HAS BEEN REPORTED ACROSS RURAL CASS COUNTY. THE FLOODING HAS BEEN DESCRIBED AS THE WORST EVER OBSERVED IN MANY AREAS. THE FLOODING IS WORST IN AREAS NEAR THE MAPLE . . . RUSH . . . AND SHEYENNE RIVERS. THIS INCLUDES LOCATIONS FROM MAPLETON TO HARWOOD.

INTERSTATE 29 NORTH OF FARGO NORTH DAKOTA TO HIGHWAY 200A SOUTH OF HILLSBORO IS CLOSED UNTIL FURTHER NOTICE DUE TO WATER LEVELS MAKING VEHICLE TRAFFIC IMPOSSIBLE ON THE INTERSTATE.

A FEW OTHER AREAS EXPERIENCING OVERLAND FLOODING INCLUDE THE SHELDON AREA OF RANSOM COUNTY AND THE COGSWELL AREA IN SARGENT COUNTY.

NORTHWEST WINDS OF 20 TO 30 MPH WILL CONTINUE TONIGHT AND RESULT IN SIGNIFICANT WAVE ACTION ON FLOODED FIELDS AND SWOLLEN RIVERS ACROSS THE AREA. WAVES OF 1 TO 2

FEET IN HEIGHT WILL BE COMMON. THE WAVES MAY CAUSE ERO-
SION OF CLAY LEVEES AND SANDBAG DIKES. THE WIND COULD
CAUSE EVEN MORE WATER TO FLOW OVER EAST TO WEST ORI-
ENTED ROADWAYS AND COULD RESULT IN ADDITIONAL EROSION
OF ROAD BEDS AND ACCELERATION OF ROAD WASHOUTS.

RESIDENTS SHOULD REMAIN VIGILANT AND MONITOR WATER
LEVELS THROUGHOUT THE AFFECTED AREAS.

PRECAUTIONARY/PREPAREDNESS ACTIONS . . .

TURN AROUND . . . DONT DROWN. AVOID DRIVING ON FLOOD-
ED ROADS. MOST FLOOD RELATED DEATHS OCCUR IN AUTOMO-
BILES.

—The Weather Channel Alert/National Weather Service

Short-Hop Notebook

Fame

April 1, 2011
In-forum.com
FARGO—It's official, at least in the eyes of online voters: Fargo is "America's Toughest Weather City."

The Weather Channel announced this morning that Fargo beat Bradford, Pa., to win the 64-city tournament.

Fargo survived a late surge by Bradford supporters to win the crown, receiving about 54 percent of the more than 55,000 votes cast, Weather Channel meteorologist Jonathan Erdman said just before 7 a.m.

"The combination of the city's infamous blizzards, extreme cold and spring floods proved too much for Bradford, Pa. in the final," The Weather Channel stated on its website.

Fargo garnered 29,837 votes to win the title, while Bradford received 25,575 votes, for a total of 55,412 votes.

Fargo steamrolled through Grand Rapids, Mich., Marquette, Mich., International Falls, Minn., Minneapolis–St. Paul and Juneau, Alaska, to reach the championship of the tournament, a spin on NCAA March Madness.

Afternoon at the Atomic Café

Imagine a photon. Just one.

It leaves our ordinary sun, and for a little bit more than eight minutes, an eternity at the atomic level, it soars through outer space. It could be visible light. It could be an X-ray, a gamma ray, an ultraviolet packet. It doesn't matter. It has the properties of a particle. It has the properties of a wave. It is, according to the textbooks, an elementary particle that is its own antiparticle, a quantum of electromagnetic energy.

Eight minutes at the speed of light. Eight minutes to cross the orbits of Mercury and Venus. And then it reaches Earth. It bounces and, with the billions of others on the same arc, it scatters and reflects and refracts and dances all over the place. And let's imagine this one photon is part of the light that is bouncing, right now, off the page and into your eye. Zip, right past your lens to the rods and cones.

Then gone. Poof. The light is absorbed. You can see the page, the ink, the letters forming words forming sentences that become the idea of this photon, but the photon is gone. More or less. Almost gone. See, the nifty thing here is that the energy never goes away. It does not diminish or lessen or weaken. The energy value of that photon is now in your body. It's powering the firing of the synapses. It's keeping you warm. That energy is changed to heat. That one little bit of light is now the physics of an idea. And, for just a moment, let's call that idea *curiosity.*

I learned this from a physicist named Heidi Manning. There is a sign on her office door that reads: "Why yes, I *am* a rocket scientist." She teaches at the college where I teach, where she is famous for her work with NASA and the Cassini Space Probe. In the basement of her building she also has a dust accelerator, one of the very few machines that can hurl micron-size particles at detectors that can tell you how the skin of the space shuttle will react when it hits dust in space or how the chemistry of the surface of the moon will change when it runs into those same particles.

"Cassini," she once said, "is a spacecraft that's going around Saturn. There are twelve different instruments on an orbiter. I worked on one that is measuring chemical composition of the gases and dust, and it also picks up ions and neutrals. It's a mass spectrometer. It takes the gas that comes in and analyzes the spectrum of masses. It has to fly through the stuff and take a sample."

I am jealous as hell. Not of the fame, or the machines, but of the way of looking at the universe. Of the level of detail. I see a picture from the Hubble telescope and feel my soul gasp at the beauty. Stars! Nebulae! Galaxies! I know what I'm looking at. I have no idea what I'm seeing at all.

There are moments, moments in the act of travel, moments of poetry and pleasure and joy and heat, that I think a physicist can explain. In particular, I want to talk about departure. I have this feeling that there is a way of looking at the act of beginning, of setting out, of pressing the gas pedal in a car, or pushing an airplane throttle to the wall, lifting a clean hiking boot out over the first step on a muddy trail, that has its roots in something much deeper than individual psychology or cultural ideas of travel. It is, I believe, much deeper than genetic. It has something to do with the way the whole universe works.

So we meet at a place called Atomic Coffee, a coffeehouse that also serves wine and beer. I order a beer, Heidi orders a smoothie, and we sit out front, watching the traffic go by. Every car and truck and bicycle is a thousand examples of her world at work. All I want her to do is explain the reason for everything.

"Would it be fair to say physics is the science of motion?" I ask.

"I would think it's more than motion," she says. "One segment describes motion. I'd say it's the science of energy. It's a way of describing the physical universe we live in."

"Okay. Let me throw a scene at you and see how you would describe it as a physicist."

"Go for it."

"When I'm sitting in an airplane, as pilot or passenger, big plane or small, there is a moment when the throttle goes forward and you can hear the engines rev or spool up, and there is that moment before the airplane catches up to the energy being pushed out the back. I know it's acceleration and momentum and all the other stuff. But there is that imbalance that the airplane tries to correct. If you were asked to describe that, from a physicist's point of view, what's happening?"

"Inertia," she says. "It basically wants to stay in the state it's in. The airplane wants to stay where it is."

"The airplane wants?"

"Yes. But I would think of it in terms of an energy transfer. I mean, the term *momentum* is often misused in everyday language, or it's used differently in everyday language from what physicists would say. To a physicist, momentum is the mass times the velocity. How fast something is moving multiplied by how much it weighs."

"That doesn't explain the feeling I get."

"Not by itself, no. I mean, oftentimes in physics there is a collision, and we talk about conservation of momentum, situations where momentum is conserved or not. As long as there are no outside forces, momentum is conserved."

"You realize that's philosophy, don't you?"

"Absolutely."

"I have this idea, and as long as no other ideas come along . . ."

"So momentum is conserved as long as nothing from the outside is pushing or pulling on it. You can stand on a frozen lake and throw an object, and as long as there is no friction or wind or anything, the object goes one way and you go the other. Momentum is conserved. Okay, so, you could look at this in terms of momentum. The exhaust from the jet comes out one way, and you go the other."

"That still doesn't get at the notion I'm chasing. When the engine goes up but you're not moving yet. That feeling of everything *about* to happen, *about* to change."

"I would think a more useful way to describe the takeoff would be an energy transfer. Your fuel is stored-up chemical potential energy. Within the engine you're going to change that chemical potential energy into something useful, the combustion process, which changes it into heat, the expansion of gases, which causes the pistons to turn and then the blades to turn. The spinning of the blades that moves the air that pushes the airplane."

"I like that," I say. "That seems closer to what I feel."

"That's the whole idea of physics that I like," Heidi says. "The energy is never created or destroyed; it just changes form."

"Tell me about acceleration, then. Because when that throttle goes forward, the plane is still sitting still. Is there a ratio or a constant or something that says for X amount of energy, acceleration would increase by a certain percentage? I mean, in that moment there is that feeling not of potential energy but of *potential*. You feel it. Every person in the airplane feels it."

"Yep. I think that is the inertia. That is the desire of something to stay in place. You have to overcome the friction, the mass. The airplane sitting on the runway has a mass. Think of mass and inertia as the same thing."

"You are using terms from psychology to describe physical processes," I say. "*Wanting. Desire.*"

"Yes," Heidi says, smiling. "I am."

"So you'd argue that what we're feeling is *resistance*? What we're feeling is the plane *wanting* to stay still?"

"Yeah, it's the resistance to motion. It's the reverse when you land—the plane wants to keep going, and you have to make it stop. So you're sitting there, and until you have enough force of that engine—you know it's kinda like I can push on this book. I can push on it and nothing happens. I'm still pushing on it. Until I push hard enough, until I get enough force, and then the book moves. You have to get your engines cranked up enough to apply enough force to overcome the friction basically between the airplane and the runway."

"Is it possible to perceive or measure something other than resistance?" I ask.

There is a pause in the conversation. Cars go by; a bird lands in a nearby shrub.

"You mean the friction?" she asks.

"Whether it's the inertia or anything—from creating an imbalance in air pressure that allows you to sip on a smoothie or the scatterings in a supercollider. Can we measure anything other than resistance?"

Another pause. A new term, and slightly different idea. A loud motorcycle goes by, followed by a silent hybrid.

"You *will* be held accountable for your answer," I laugh.

"Yeah, well, I hadn't thought about it in terms of resistance." You can tell when a new idea is playing, doing cartwheels and jumping jacks in a person's head.

"I've always thought, in an airplane, when I do feel that rush, I do feel the press against my back of the seat. Which is the inertia. My body is resisting the seat moving forward until there is enough pressure, and I move forward too. But there is this whole notion of anticipation as well."

"So you're thinking about *resistance*?" she asks.

"As you were talking, it seemed to me a life spent perceiving resistance can be either tremendously depressing or a great opportunity for understanding. Everything I see is in contrast to something else. Everything I see is change. Everything I see is resisting some prior perception."

The idea hangs there, midair, lingering.

I decide to make sure I've got the terms right.

"What is the definition of *acceleration*?" I ask.

"A change in velocity that happens over time. Acceleration is caused by outside forces."

"What is *force*?"

"Anything that pushes or pulls."

"*Work*?"

"Change in energy that happens over time."

"Wait. Energy isn't created or destroyed. How is that possible?"

"Change in the amount of energy."

"Does an airplane *work* itself into the sky?"

"I wouldn't say that. I would say that work is done. Work is done on the airplane that causes it to go into the sky. You know, I do work here." She lifts her smoothie into the air. "I'm doing work against gravity. So if I have my smoothie up in the air, it has potential energy because it's up at some height. Where did that energy come from? It came from the work I did. It came from my giving it some kinetic energy to move it to a new height."

"And the relationship of gravity to that is?"

"The amount of work done is equal to the change in potential energy. So the amount of work I did in lifting this is equal to the energy difference between on the table and above the table. So how much did its potential energy change? Potential energy, gravitational potential energy, depends on height. So if I want to lift something up, I have to change its potential energy; I have to do work on it. So in that sense I'm changing the energy of that thing."

"So it's *not* by works alone then," I quip.

"Now," she continues, "the energy is not being created. It's just being *transferred* to that thing. From me. From the energy I got from *drinking* the smoothie, I was able to *lift* the smoothie."

I suddenly wish I had a picture. Two people, sitting at a metal table on a summer afternoon, one of them holding a smoothie above her head, and the whole mechanism of the universe is unveiled.

"I was thinking about your resistance question," she says. "Is what you're talking about just Newton's first law? 'An object in motion stays in motion unless there is an outside force. An object at rest stays at rest unless there is an outside force.' You know, basically, does it want to change? You have to push or pull to make it change. You have to apply that force. I often think about it in terms of everyday life, too. You know, things are going smoothly; you don't want things to change; you have to apply some force to make a change happen. For good or for bad."

"Resistance equals perception? Resistance equals perspective?"

"Perhaps."

"Tell me more about exploring Saturn," I say. "What's in it for you?"

"It is a better way to understand the earth," she says. "Where we live. What processes happen here, by going out and getting more data points. With the technology we have, we're never going to go anywhere beyond our solar system. We're stuck in our neighborhood. So what can we learn better and more about our neighborhood, who is in our neighborhood, how did it come to be? So why explore the other planets? What do I enjoy about it? It's getting more pieces for the puzzle. How did our solar system come to be? How did it evolve? How did this moon, Titan, get created where it is? Why does it have an atmosphere? What's in the atmosphere of that moon? Why is it out at that distance? How did it *get* out there? How did Saturn get to be at that spot? We know it didn't form at that spot. It migrated to that spot. Jupiter migrated in as well. We know these things based on the composition of what's out there—what is it made out of? How did it come to be? You know, we always used to think the big gas giants had to be far out in a solar system. But then you start exploring and you find extrasolar planets, and there are hundreds of gas giants really close in. Why are the other solar systems different from ours? So our theory about how the planets formed has to change because we have more data points."

"Are you more excited by confirmation," I ask, "or by the unexpected?"

"I don't know. I think more of the unexpected."

"So when you find something in your work, and you think that's wrong or that shouldn't be there . . ."

"I'm thinking of a very simple, trivial thing. On the Cassini probe, the instrument we were working with is measuring the chemical composition of the atmosphere of Titan. Titan is a moon that's going around Saturn. It's the only moon with a substantial atmosphere. And it's got a lot of interesting chemistry going on there. We had models of what the chemical composition of this moon's atmosphere would be like."

"Based on telescopes?"

"Yeah, so we kinda knew some of the big components. There's nitrogen. There's methane. We knew these things would be in the atmosphere already. But what are some of the trace elements, where are they located, how are they layered? This sort of thing. One of the unusual things we found was that there's benzene, which is a fairly complex hydrocarbon, heavy mass, a lot of carbon, a lot of hydrogen, big molecule. And it's really high up in the atmosphere. Nobody predicted that it would be up there. I mean, some people predicted it might be in the atmosphere, but it would definitely be closer to the surface. It wouldn't be up really high. So why are we finding this big molecule up there? So that's the unexpected."

"Okay, why is benzene way up high in the atmosphere there?"

"We don't know. We measured it. A couple of my good friends are 'chemical theorists,' if you will—they do the modeling of the atmosphere—and I joke with them and say my job is to keep you honest. You can make a model and predict *whatever*, and you think this is the way it's going to be. And all of a sudden we take some data, and now you have to change your model because it doesn't agree with reality. You have some nice ideas, but there are limitations, and maybe you need to tweak something or you need to change the parameters of your model because we're finding something you didn't predict. That's the unexpected. We didn't expect to find this much chemistry going on. We thought, you know, in the earth's atmosphere all the interesting chemistry is down low. When you get up, it's just hydrogen and helium and atomic oxygen. It kind of separates out and it's not real interesting. It's just kind of separated out by mass, and there you go. Titan has a lot more interesting stuff going on, and how does that work?

"Science is a process," she continues. "It's a way of asking and answering questions. And you can never know for certain. We have Newton's laws of gravity that say this thing is going to fall and hit the ground, and I've got a pretty good idea that that's going to happen. Newton's laws of gravity explain a lot, but they're not perfect. Einstein came along with his ideas of general relativity, and we had to make some changes. Newton is an approximation on a big scale."

"Is physics a branch of philosophy?" I ask.

"I would say. It started out historically that way. Physics is natural philosophy. And as you get more into it and think more deeply about the physics—I mean, there's the Physics 101, understanding the macroscopic world, and describing the motion of this object going down the street or this object going up in the air, whatever. You're describing mathematically the things you observe. But as you start getting more and more into it, and closer to the theory and the unknown, it really starts to mesh with the philosophy. I think the more that you study it, the more you see it's not just the facts and apply this formula to get the answer. Some people think that's what physics is."

"There has to be a moment," I say, "in your life and in other physicists' lives, when you discover the benzene in completely the wrong place, and you don't go to your calculator or your computer, but you basically sit down with a good glass of chardonnay and you think what the hell is that doing up there?"

"Exactly."

"It becomes a creative art."

"Yep. Yep. What was I missing before? I'm missing something in my understanding of that process because I didn't get it all. It's the creative process then, and that goes back to your earlier question—is the joy in the confirmation or the discovery of something new? And that's where I think it's more energizing to have the new discoveries and the unexpected because it promotes the creativity."

Yes, I think. This sounds right. There is a moment, at the beginning of every departure, which holds the universe. Momentum and inertia and acceleration and resistance and the transfer of energy and the hum of every atom wanting, desiring, leading us to wonder.

Ground Reference

Last night, like so many nights before, I drew a line on a sectional chart. Fargo, North Dakota, to the Coteau des Prairies, a range of hills just over the border in South Dakota. Seventy-three nautical miles on a heading of 190 degrees from home.

I've seen those hills a thousand times from the ground. Driving up and down Interstate 29, I've seen those hills rise on the western horizon, a pretty break on the flatland prairie, and I know just enough about geology to have wondered—why are those hills there? Today I have a partial answer, and so I want to see them again. I want to see them from the air.

I cannot remember what I was trying to find, but while surfing through Wikipedia one night, a picture showed up on the edge of my computer screen.

It was a tangent at best. But this was a picture of home and it implied a story, so I spent some time reading. In truth, the Coteau des Prairies is just a pile of dirt pushed up into a moraine by a prehistoric ice sheet. That ice receded. When the next ice came, however, the famous Laurentide ice sheet, the Coteau des Prairies, refused to move. It split the glacier and caused a deeper gouging of the land on each side. The hills are nothing spectacular, remarkable only because they are completely out of place, yet they even show up on the maps of Lewis and Clark (*center, top*), called the Mountain on the Prairie.

What I really want to see today is invisible. From the left seat of a rented Cessna 172, heading south toward those rising hills, I want to see history. I want to see the force of the Laurentide ice sheet moving down the continent, and I want to see the hills split the ice. Imagine the slip of paper in a theater program: "Tonight the part of the very large glacier will be played by a very

small airplane." You could call it a type of situational awareness. I want to know, as richly as possible, where I am.

There is a wonderful quote by writer Reg Saner. "Destination," he says, "is mere pretext for the real business of going to meet it." The reason we practice and refine the grace of our landings, the reason we calculate wind-correction angles and time between waypoints, is that the joy of holding a machine in the sky is profound. The more we know about the land we're crossing, the deeper that joy becomes.

In summer, the approach to the International Peace Garden airport (S28) is calendar-art beautiful. Prairie farmland gives way to deep-green forest near the Canadian border. Round hay bales and ponds dot the fields heading into Runway 28. It's an easy landing, and the gardens are worth the trip. The poutine in the café is very good.

There is a famous glitch in Flight Simulator here. For whatever reason, in the computer world a giant chasm opens on the far end of the runway, and you can fly nearly thirty thousand feet down toward the center of the earth. There is no such hole in real life, but there is something underground. You cannot see it from the air, and you cannot see it on the ground, even if you're looking for it hard. But one look at a gravity map shows this part of the state has some of the densest rock possible. Landing at the Peace Garden, it seems, is landing on the summit of an underground mountain.

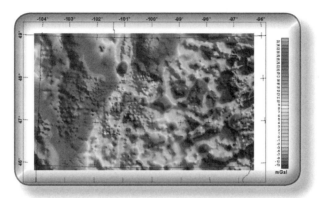

It makes a difference in the way you understand where you are. The North Dakota Isostatic Gravity Anomaly Map isn't hard to find. Just Google "North Dakota Gravity Map." Better yet, Google whatever state you live in. Along the same lines, ever wonder why sectionals sometimes warn about extreme magnetic variations? There is something called an aeromagnetic anomaly map.

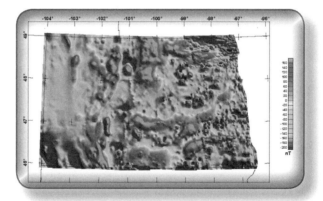

It all makes a difference. Long Island is a different place if you know the whole thing is a moraine pushed up by a glacier. The Grand Canyon is a different place if you know the Colorado River isn't cutting down as much as the land is rising up, and the sight out your side of the airplane is more impressive if you've spent a moment with a map of the canyon wall and learned about the Great Unconformity. The Ozarks are different when you understand the hills used to be mountains that used to be an island in the midst of a Paleozoic sea.

I remember learning ground reference—*S* turns over a county road, turns around a point over some farmstead in the practice area. Back then, the road and the farmstead didn't really matter. They were arbitrary choices, references to use while I learned to muscle or finesse the airplane, to get ahead of the airplane and winds. Once I knew what I was doing, I wanted to know who traveled that road. I wanted to know who lived in that house.

One thing leads to another. Thirteen of the lower forty-eight states have impact craters left by meteorites. A map will show you the Manson Crater in Iowa, a hole large enough that scientists first thought this might be the site of the dinosaur-killer asteroid until the Yucatán site was discovered. You cannot see the Manson Crater—it was filled in long ago—but you'll see it's not very far from Madison County. The bridges of Madison County *can* be seen from the air, and they are lovely.

We use our sectionals and approach charts. We use maps of winds aloft and maps of bad weather. We use maps of how our airplanes will behave (though we call them performance charts). We are experts with the maps that get us safely from takeoff to landing.

There are maps only a few of us ever see. FalconView, for example, is a version of the standard sectionals used by Department of Defense (DOD) pilots. It's not secret; it's just not available to GA (general aviation) pilots. A government pilot once showed me an interesting bit of information on his map that was nowhere on mine.

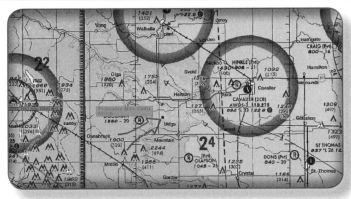

My sectional does not say the buildings are an over-the-horizon radar site, but FalconView has a note-taking feature. The warning is nothing official. It's just a bit of experience the pilots entered into their system. When I asked if there was any reason I should avoid this site as well, the answer was *probably* not.

Back at home, I looked at an expired sectional. There was no reason, I thought, I couldn't write my own notes. I got out my log book and drew a line for every flight. I wrote "weekend sailboat races" next to Cormorant Lake, "fly fishing for brown trout" next to the Straight River, "Continental Divide" between the James and Sheyenne Rivers. And yes, I wrote "Perimeter Area Radar: Avoid!" next to the buildings west of Cavalier.

If I have a story, a bit of personal history or local lore, I write it on an old sectional. If I have a desire for some future flight, that goes on the old map too. My friend Mike Paulson has promised to show me the interlake paddleboat trail in western Minnesota. I've promised myself the path of the Pony Express.

Sometimes the places we desire appear like Brigadoon overnight and disappear just as quickly. On the morning television weather report, we often see maps of last night's rain- or snowstorm, maps of storm totals and locations. Not so long ago, the map showed two and a half inches of rain from a Memorial Day storm just north of town.

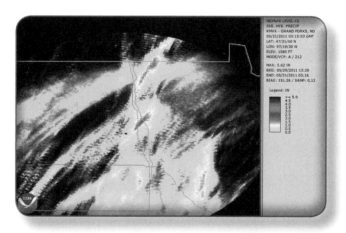

I really had nowhere to go. But I wanted some time in the air and a new place to visit. One inch of rain over one acre of land weighs more than 113 tonnes. This storm dropped 283 tonnes of water per acre. That's 67,885 gallons of water per acre. The next morning I was fifteen hundred feet AGL, following the rain paths, amazed.

The Coteau des Prairies rises in front of me, brown and green and beautiful in early-fall daylight. The leaves on the trees are turning, and we are just past first frost. I fly low, and from here I can easily imagine the advancing glaciers, the push and the resistance and then the breaking into two. The map in the G1000 is almost irrelevant today. Because of a different map, I know I am flying over the bed of Pleistocene Lake Agassiz. Because of different maps, I know the annual rainfall and population density. I know what types of rock rest under the soil and what crops were planted this year.

You could call it situational awareness. The earth is simply more beautiful, and flying more rewarding, when you understand more deeply where you are. "Destination," he said, "is mere pretext for the real business of going to meet it."

Short-Hop Notebook

Stats

"The continental U.S. averages about 11 blizzards a year with the worst occurring in the upper plains," he said. *"The Red River Valley in eastern North Dakota and western Minnesota has the most recorded blizzards in the last four decades."*

Counties in the Red River Valley average more than one blizzard each year with the annual probability of such a storm occurring at least 63 percent of the time. Fargo, N.D., has the highest probability rate at 76 percent with Grand Forks, N.D., at 71 percent and Minneapolis at 54 percent.

—Ball State University News Center

Storm Flying

On the prairie, it is possible to lie on your back under the summertime sky and believe the only thing between you and a beautiful truth are some cotton-ball clouds. Killdeer and red-wing blackbirds sound near a pond. A mourning dove calls from a rooftop. Swallows wheel overhead, while robins search for worms. There is a small breeze in the tops of the ash and maple trees, and it all seems so open, so empty, so inviting, and so easy.

Nothing could be further from the truth.

In Minot, North Dakota, where more than eleven thousand people are leaving town today, evacuating in response to the flooding Souris River, ancient and lethal B-52 bombers still rumble out of the air base on training missions and patrol. Nuclear bombs are stored on-site. From the air base in Grand Forks, UAVs (unmanned aerial vehicles) and drones leap into the sky west of town, their pilots learning the trick of flying an airplane remotely, while at the University of North Dakota students from all over the planet learn how to fly, the Dakota radio waves thick with the accents of their homelands. And up high, jets on their way to Minneapolis from Japan, Korea, Hawaii, and Alaska throttle back and begin their descents over prairie wheat, canola, sunflowers, and sugar beets.

It is not a congested sky, but it is a complicated picture. And then there are storms. Big, fat, kick-your-ass storms in every season. Blizzards in winter. Straight-line windstorms in springtime and fall. Thunderstorms in summer. Thunderstorms with battlefield lightning, crop-shredding hail, and tornadoes. Sometimes the thunderstorms are dry and the lightning sets the prairie grass on fire. Sometimes the rain is so hard, whole buildings go missing. If you are a pilot, and especially the pilot of a small airplane, you do anything to avoid these storms. The wind, the ice, the violence of the sky can shake you out of your wits and out of the sky.

Hans Ahlness makes his living flying into thunderstorms. He convinces other pilots to do the same thing. He is the vice president of operations for Weather Modification, Inc., a part of the Fargo Jet Center, with clients in Antigua, Argentina, Australia, Burkina Faso, Canada, Greece, India, Indonesia, Jordan, Mali, Mexico, Morocco, Saudi Arabia, Senegal, Spain, Thailand, Turkey, the United Arab Emirates, and the United States.

"I grew up in the company," he says. "Literally. I grew up in a town called Bowman, North Dakota, down in the southwest corner of the state—that's where the company started—and I lived across the street from Wilbur Brewer, the owner. When I was a little airport rat, I used to ride my monkey bike out to the airport, and every time there was a storm I would ride out and watch the radar and watch the airplanes take off and land. So when I needed a summer job in high school I went to talk to Wilbur, figuring I'd be driving a grain truck or swather or something, and instead I became an assistant in the radar. I started doing that when I was sixteen, then I went to college and did all my flying and came back and flew in the summers. I've been full-time since 1985."

Hans and I are sitting in the lounge outside the Weather Modification offices. I want to know what it's like to fly into a thunderstorm. I've tried to arrange a ride, but there are a thousand good reasons—most of them having to do with law and Federal Aviation Administration regulations—I cannot score a seat. So I am asking for stories. I am asking about storms.

"When you learn to fly," he says, "you're taught to stay the heck away from them."

Hans looks like a football player, a linebacker maybe, and he talks with his hands. Not wildly, but expressively—lifting and pointing and curving his words.

"Stay twenty miles away from cells. Don't fly between them," he continues. "And all that's right. The weather gets bad around here. You get turbulence. You get wind shear. You get lower visibility from extra cloudiness or rain. You get windshields broken out due to hail. You can get hit by lightning. Doesn't happen very often down low, but it can happen. Lots of bad stuff can happen around here. So what we have to do is teach our guys how to safely operate in the area in close to the storm, where you're not supposed to be."

"Is it technically difficult?" I ask. "Is it difficult to do the flying you do? I mean, the ride might do a number with your kidneys and spleen. But is the flying very hard?"

"It isn't," he says. "No."

"You're kidding."

"Well," he says, drawing out the word, "not so much. The most danger-ous part is still the takeoff and landing. You're down close to the ground, and you're flying around thunderstorms where there's going to be shifting winds. Generally, the airplanes are going to be working in front of a thunderstorm, flying in front of it as it moves across. That's where the inflow generally is. So say they're low on fuel or they're running out of chemical, and they need to land to rearm. And one of the spots for them to land is in front of the storm. In front of a storm, you generally have a gust front. Or if it's a front coming through, you have strong winds in front of the front. Either way, that's a bad combination for landing. And the same thing for the back. If you're going to duck through the storm, get beat up a little bit, and then land behind the storm, there's all the turbulence and downflows behind a storm as well. It's like a ship just passed and the water's rolling."

Outside the windows of the lounge, I can see a Supercub start up and taxi toward takeoff. A student and instructor pull up in a Cessna 172. A regional jet takes off for a trip to Denver. The afternoon is low overcast but calm.

"One of your pilots," I say, "has a picture of flying just with a gust front."

"Oh, it's beautiful," Hans says.

"Do you fly through that stuff?" I ask.

"At cloud base, we are always VFR [visual flight rules]. If we're seeding the tops of the feeder cells, which is really just midlevel in the storm, we might fly through stuff. But not when we're working the base. I've noticed the younger guys pick on bigger stuff, bigger feeder cells, than us older guys. And I under-stand. When I was younger, I'd fly into a cell that was already five or ten thou-sand feet above me and young me would say, 'Whew! That's a good ride!' Now, old me knows I'm going to get my headset beat into the top of my head, and there's already ice in there, and I'm probably going to run into hail, and it's too big for what I want to do."

"Walk me through a normal flight?" I ask. "I mean, it's not like you're a fire-man. The alarm bell doesn't go off, and you don't go sliding down poles, and you don't turn on the sirens and flashing lights. But this is pretty on-call stuff. If you're going to seed a thunderstorm, those can build pretty fast."

"Let's just talk North Dakota," he says. "There are two radars out in the western part of the state. Both are owned by the state, and both are operated by state meteorologists. All our airplanes and pilots are based out near there. Bowman, Williston, Watford City, Stanley and Kenmare and Minot. Every-body's always on-call weather watch. If there are storms growing in Montana, we're watching them. Depending on the forecast, you might be on standby or alert. 'Alert' means you're sitting at the airport ready to go. Now radar doesn't see a thunderstorm until it already has rain in it. Radar sees precipitation, not clouds. And if we're dealing with a hailstorm, which grows fast, by the time the radar sees it, it may be past the point where we can work. So a lot of the stuff that we're flying in isn't going to be on the ground-based radar. So you need to be there before you're needed—that kind of thing.

"The state guys are looking at the radar and at satellite pictures, and we're watching and we see cumulous growing. So they call me or I call them. Either way. We preflighted the airplane after its last flight, so it's always ready to go. And then away we go. We're going to fly to where the area of new growth is, which is generally on the south side. And lots of times on the southeast side of the storm, you'll see a shelf cloud. You're looking for a smooth, flat base. You don't want to be in the rain shaft. You've got to be out in front of it. And you don't want to be underneath the shelf cloud, because that's a shear zone. Generally, there's another base above the shelf cloud, and you want to work the edges out in front of that. That's where the inflow is. You want an inflow of five hundred to eight hundred feet a minute, because in the eight to ten minutes it takes for your chemicals to become active, those fake ice crystals get up into the area of the storm where there is supercooled liquid water, which will cause it all to make more ice crystals and rain out earlier than it would have otherwise."

"Tell me a story?" I ask. "Is there one storm, or three?"

Hans pauses, hands in his lap.

"Every storm is different," he says. "But you've seen it from the ground. A big hailstorm is coming, and it's green. Deep green. Well, when you're flying right next to it, that green color, which we always figure is bad because it means there's a crapload of water and ice in there, is just crystal clear. There's no dust. No trees or anything. No pollution. The colors are just intensified. And the lightning—you get a good show with that. Sometimes, at night—I can remember flying a really big storm one night out of Bowman. Huge cells. Big shelf cloud. I was out in front to the east. Ten-mile-wide flat base. And it was just like a concrete deck above me, it was so flat. And there was so much lightning coming out of it, we'd duck inside the airplane. You don't hear thunder inside an airplane unless it's close, and we were hearing thunder all the time. It was like they were shooting at us, almost. It gets your attention. Then it started hailing, and we had to bail out of that area. But everything was so sharply defined.

"There was another storm—about two in the morning, but so much lightning it was just like daytime. There was a tornado out of that one. The guys working the ground radar bailed out and went to someone's basement in town. It was so intense. There was no dome over the radar, and the dish wouldn't turn in the wind, so they were blind anyway. Every feeder we went into the updrafts was so severe the storm would literally just throw us back out. We'd come out of the cell in a 90-degree toss. Not in a turn. Not at a bank or anything. We were just thrown that direction out of the cell. And you get to where you think you don't want to do that again! That was the roughest beating I'd ever taken."

"Is it satisfying?" I ask.

Hans smiles a deep smile.

"Well, the scenery in a thunderstorm can't be beat. But the thing about storm flying," he says, "is you don't necessarily know where you're going, and you don't know where you're going to end up, and you don't know how long you're going to be gone. So you're always making it up as you go. Dealing with the situation. And that is, to me—fun. A hell of a lot of fun."

Short-Hop Notebook

Jazz

Imagine a funky drum and a syncopated bass, slap bass, a horn section in the background. Think of a sax playing way down low, a throaty sound with a hum put in—what a sax player would call a growl. And imagine the crescendo toward that one impossible note way up high. Then the release, a move into cut time, a race toward home.

Now imagine an airplane, call sign One Two Whiskey, one thousand five hundred feet above the prairie, in a hard bank to the left. It's called a steep turn. To maintain altitude, the pilot pulls back on the yoke and the g-load increases. You can feel your ass get planted in the seat. Imagine the turn changing from hard left to hard right. Sixty-degree bank angle. Like standing the airplane on the wingtip. Hold it there. Release and turn again to the left. Sweeping S turns over the prairie, just to feel the airplane sing. Pull back on the yoke until the airplane stalls. Or cut power and glide, nearly silent, only a flute still soft in the hall.

It really is like that sometimes.

Tag

I remember the running.
Usually twilight, or later.
You're it.
Now run.
Chase.
Reach.
Feel that touch.
Run.
Turn.
Bank.
Dodge.
You're it.
Now run.
Just run.
Reach and run some more.
Nothing to win or lose.
Just the speed of the chase.
The adrenaline joy of running hard and turning sharp.
Your hand on someone's arm or back or shoulder or head changes every-
thing.
Tag.
You're it.
Now run.

Game on, I think. We are cleared for takeoff, and as I move the throttle forward, I can feel the familiar, wonderful press of a seat against my back. We are rolling, pointed west, heading down Runway Two-Seven. The airspeed indicator moves past 60 knots, I pull back on the wheel, and somewhere in my body I can feel that moment when the airplane lifts easily into a warm and clear July morning on the northern prairie. Run, I think. Reach. We are off to Rugby, North Dakota, to tag the geographical center of North America. Just to touch it, to press a hand to the stone, to say we are here. Even though it's not really there.

The airplane is a Cessna 172. Tail number: N6065M. Six-Five Mike. In the seat next to me, Tim Megorden, the pastor at the college where I teach, looks out the window as the ground recedes and the horizon leaps toward the huge. He loves to fly and has been asking for a ride. Who better to take to the middle of something?

"Oh, what a beautiful morning," I sing, enthusiastically, fully off-key, not opening the microphone but loud enough for the intercom to work.

"Did you sing for the choir?" he asks.

"Yeah, can't you tell?"

Below us, the landscape north and west of Fargo, North Dakota, quickly becomes cropland. Small grains and sugar beets. Sunflowers and canola. Section roads divide the farms into neat squares. Shelterbelts run just as straight, protection from the wind here that humbles mountaineers. Field and forest and riverbank. Every field is green, though there are a hundred variations. Yellow green. Emerald green. Neon green. First-car green. Bad-sweater green. Chocolate green.

"This is smooth," Tim says.

I know he's talking about the air. We are early enough in this day the thermals have yet to get going, and even though there's a wind, coming straight at us, slowing us down a bit, it passes easily over the wings. But I agree for the other reason. We are two thousand feet above the ground, motoring through the morning, able to see a larger version of this day no one on the ground will know. Yes, I think, this is smooth.

I hand Tim a small camera.

"What do you want me to take pictures of?" he asks.

"Any kind of panorama," I say. "Anything at all."

Run.

Chase.

Reach.

Three is good. Seven is better. You need a crowd for a good game of tag. You need to have that wonder—who is he really chasing? You run and the whole world weaves away. You are the center of everything, and everyone reacts to you. You make a choice and give it your best shot, but even then another choice comes into range. You change course, surprise everyone. Your hand hits an elbow or thigh. Tag. The center shifts. Star becomes satellite. You're it. Now run.

Like all the good trips, this one began with a simple wondering. I was reading about a very young sailor, alone in the southeastern Pacific Ocean, passing what is called Point Nemo. Just a bit of math, really. Point Nemo is the spot farthest from any land, sitting in unbroken water between New Zealand and South America, a bit more than sixteen hundred miles in any direction from any soil. The very middle of nowhere, I thought. Unless you're an oceanographer, which would make it the very middle of everywhere. Tough to get there, I thought.

Then I was hooked. North Pole, South Pole, Equator, Everest, Marianas Trench—those are easy. Those are the edges. But where are the middles? By definition, a middle is the average farthest away from more than one edge. The middle of the earth's population is somewhere in India. Zero latitude meets zero longitude under the water of the Atlantic off the coast of Africa. The encyclopedia lists the Poles of Inaccessibility—those places that are farthest from other places. Point Nocean, in the Xinjiang region of China, is the farthest from any ocean. The island farthest away from other land is Bouvet Island in the South Atlantic.

Yet there are problems. None of this is real in the way that a peak or a valley is real. The measurements depend upon assumptions. If I am looking for the center of my house, do I count the garage? If I am looking for the center of the earth, do I go by average sea level, or do I include Everest? There is no center to the universe. What we learned in school is true. The speed and position of any object depend on the speed and position of the observer, unless we're talking about the speed of light, which is constant.

To declare a middle says almost nothing about the place itself and quite a lot about the act of declaration. Tag, I thought. You're it.

"What towns will we be flying over?" Tim asks.

I point to the moving map on the instrument panel, the little picture of an airplane and a line from us straight to Rugby. Town names appear on the left and right. Arthur. Page. Colegate. Galesburg. Hope. Cooperstown. Jessie. Binford. I tell him I have a paper chart too, if he wants to follow along. But the names are enough, and his eyes return to the prairie under the wings.

A large radio tower goes by on the right.

"Can you imagine building that?" I ask. "It's as high as we are now."

Fields of small grains quilt their way to every compass point. Small drainages appear in the fields, wind their way toward lower ground. Canola appears, the bright-yellow crop a sharp and pretty contrast to the many shades of deep green. A wind farm appears in the distance. A semitruck heads down a gravel road, the white plume of dust rising behind him and lingering in the air.

It's the type of day where every sight is an invitation to wondering. See that town? Who lives there? See that road? I wonder what it's like to be there. Where does this one begin? Who drives it so often the grooves are more remembered than seen, and who drives it for a first time? Look at that small lake. I wonder if there are any fish.

We cross small streams and look for the Sheyenne River and Lake Ashtabula in the distance off the left side. Tim takes pictures of the meandering courses, the thick trees on each riverbank. Water, we tell each other, is a deep-rooted fascination. Ancient and genetic. On the prairie, it's the break from the straight-line section roads and crop rows. Thomas Jefferson, I say, set up the surveying that created the grids we see, but water's sense of history has nothing to do with measurement.

We are flying at three thousand feet above sea level, about one thousand eight hundred feet above the ground here, at nine on a clear Friday morning. Below us, just farmsteads and waterways, roads and windbreaks and marks on the land. Evidence of agriculture, economics, culture, settlement, transportation, politics, history, geology, hydrology, limnology, meteorology, psychology, and art. Tag, I think. Pick a target. Reach. It all could not be prettier.

I change radio frequency to hear the small airport traffic.

"The difference in color would indicate it's not as flat down there as it appears from the ground," Tim says.

"Wind is picking up," I say. "We may be in for a couple bumps."

"This is so cool, so cool," he says.

The center of North America is too good to pass, even if it's not really true. Rugby claims the title and has a monument, a stone cairn with a sign on each side that reads: "Geographical Center of North America. Rugby, ND." People stop and have their pictures taken here. Across the parking lot, at the Cornerstone Café, people buy cups of coffee, milkshakes, and hamburgers and marvel at the wonder of being in the very exact precise middle of North America. It doesn't matter that this version of the middle does not include Mexico, much less the rest of southern North America. It doesn't matter that the real center, even just considering the United States and Canada, is actually sixteen miles away, six miles west of Balta, North Dakota, population seventy-three, in the middle of a large pond. There is a marker here, something people can touch and feel and see.

Tag, I think.

I send an e-mail to two friends, extraordinary cartographers, to ask if there is an official list of center places, given all the problems with definitions.

Jon Kimerling writes:

> *Scott,*
> *The starting point for surveying the North American Datum of 1927 is a monument at Meades Ranch, Kansas in the center of the continent. The center of population for the United States has been computed for each census and the westward and southward shift over time is shown on maps.*
> *Jon*

Now this, I think, is a place to go see. I have to look it up, but the North American Datum of 1927 was nothing less than the exact measurement of a continent. It set the coordinates for everything. It was elegant math and dirty boots. Something called a Triangulation Station at Meades Ranch was zero zero, the beginning place for everything measured. Another monument. Another thing to touch and claim. (A quick look online, however, tells me there is no café and thus no coffee, milkshakes, or hamburgers.) But wait, I think. *Kansas* is the middle of the continent? Who says?

Mark Monmonier's e-mail comes next:

> *Hi Scott,*
> *I haven't thought much of the significance of places recognized as geographic centers or extrema. It's probably human nature to try to capitalize on any point of notoriety. I'm curious in particular about the mathematical stability of some of these places, including issues of how distance is calculated (on the sphere or on an ellipsoid, and if so, which one) and how the reference space is defined (especially if there are outliers that might spin the outcome). What's included in a continent, for instance? For the US, what do we do about Alaska and Hawaii? And then there's the issue of center of population vis-à-vis center of land area. And what if we throw in maritime territory—the territorial sea, the contiguous area, the Exclusive Economic Zone. Doesn't the wide range of centers undermine the significance of center? I'd think so.*
> *All best,*
> *Mark*

Exactly, I think. But damn, what fun is that? Grain elevators and farmsteads and power lines go by below us. The wind farm north of Valley City grows closer, nearly every blade turning. On the radio, someone says, "Man, it's just gorgeous out here today." We are coming up on a town called Hope.

I don't care if Rugby is the real center or not. You can't win the game of tag. All you can do is play, run as hard and fast as you can, reach with the full length of your arm.

A small church appears on Tim's side. A tall steeple, a white clapboard structure, it's small and completely alone. We count section roads away from the church and run out of line of sight before we come to any town. At least ten miles in every direction.

"I would love to land there," I say. "I would love to just plunk down on that gravel road and pull up to the church, in an airplane, and get out to see who is there."

"There probably isn't any one there," Tim says.

"I know. Part of a circuit. On Sunday morning, some pastor who has three different churches to get to. He or she could live anywhere inside fifty miles of here."

"My father," Tim says, "had seven churches."

It takes me a minute to do the math.

"How in the world did he do seven churches? First one at dawn, last one at midnight?"

"He left before the service was over."

"What?"

"That was back in the day when communion was less common. Maybe once a month. After the sermon he would go out the back and get on the road to the next one. The congregation would finish up the service."

"God love the deacons," I say.

"Amen."

I have a vision of a flying-pastor service, something like the Royal Flying Doctor Service in Australia. Small airplanes at idle outside small churches, pastors in robes ducking out from behind the sanctuaries and rushing to the copilot's seat. The choir and congregation's hymn joined by the thrumming of a prop biting air and the sight of wings lifting skyward. The next church listening for a sound in the heavens, seeing the wings appear, the glint of lowered flaps in the sunshine, the appearance of a body in flowing robes. It could work. It could work really well, I think. Unless the weather was bad. Or the winds too strong.

Tim and I talk about flying. Many years ago he took lessons. Troubled eyesight keeps him from the pilot's seat now. But I cannot get the image of that church out of my head, or the image of a very small plane coming to earth in front of it. There are airplanes that can do that. Late at night, browsing airplane ads and dreaming, I have imagined flying the airplanes that specialize in short takeoff and landing. Here in Six-Five Mike, at slow cruise, we are flying faster than the top speed of most of those. It would take forever to get anywhere, but speed would not be the issue. I have imagined landing in the middle of the college campus. I have imagined landing it on the college football field, in the church parking lot next to my home, on the bike path where I walk my dog, on a thousand dirt roads I know in Minnesota, North Dakota, Kansas, Missouri, Texas. And I have imagined landing it in a thousand places I still want to visit. In Wyoming and Colorado and New Mexico. With floats attached I want to land on James Bay, Hudson Bay, Prudhoe Bay, Bay of Fundy, Lake Superior, Lake of the Ozarks, Upper Red Lake, Tablerock Lake, Lake Baikal.

To imagine an airplane is to imagine the way it lifts you into the sky and the way it places you back again. The full curved flap of an angel's wings.

Devil's Lake is a problem.

We are not there yet, but the earth below us is swelling with water. Ditches and coolies. Streams. The Maple River. The Sheyenne River. Lake Coe. Johnson Lake. Stump Lake. A thousand potholes filled with rainwater and snowmelt. It all drains to the Maple or the Sheyenne. The Maple and Sheyenne drain to the Red River. The Red River flows north, into Canada, into Lake Winnipeg, eventually into Hudson Bay.

But not Devil's Lake. Devil's Lake is a terminal lake. There is no outlet, no drain, nowhere for the lake water to go. Evaporation takes a bit, but the water continues to rise. It is higher now than at any time in record keeping. In 1940 the lake level was fourteen hundred feet above sea level. This morning as Six-Five Mike heads toward it, the level is fifty feet higher. And it can rise very fast. Fish finders on boats see hay bales still in fields now under water. Corn crops planted in spring seem to march into the sea at harvest. The lake has risen more than thirty feet since 1993, and the surface area has quadrupled. State geologists claim it's overflowed at least seven times, most recently about eighteen hundred years ago. The US Geological Survey (USGS) says our current cycle of wet weather will go on for at least another decade.

When it gets high enough, Devil's Lake will flow into Stump Lake. A little bit higher, and both flow into the Sheyenne. It's possible to build an outlet, to drain some of the lake. But Canada does not want Devil's Lake water. Canada is against the water in Devil's Lake. The town of Minnewaukan used to be eight miles from the western lakeshore. Today the village is partly flooded, and there is talk, serious talk, of moving the entire thing. The population has diminished from 318 to 260 people as the lake fills basements and yards.

Underneath the airplane now, however, fields appear with hay cut and swathed but not yet collected into bales, long, straight lines of golden feed.

"There was a slough back there," Tim says, "that actually looked like it had ripples, like someone had dredged concentric circles."

Oak and elm and ash trees line the banks of the Sheyenne River. The river turns in lazy oxbows.

"That's what I love," I say. "You see one thing and it provokes a thousand questions. It implies so many stories, all of them possible, and God, you want to know which one is true. How did those ripples get there? What did this place look like five hundred years ago? How long does it take a river like this to meander, to cut just one loop?"

"Does your mind always go to land history?" he asks.

"It goes to story," I say. "Everything is connected. See those new power lines down there? Remember the blizzards of 1997 when the old ones all froze and toppled over? What I see this morning is a new tower. Push that sight just a bit, and you uncover a huge story of very bad weather. Those birds we passed a bit back? We're on the edge here of something called the Central Flyway, a huge migration corridor for birds. Siberia to Mexico. Sandhill cranes and swans and geese and everything else. Look down there. See that one farm-stead sitting alone in that section? That home is there because of old home-steading laws. When you got the free or cheap land, the rule was you had to live on it. It was a good idea to prevent hoarding and speculation. But it also went against what most of the immigrants were used to. In Europe, you lived in town and went out each morning to your fields. When you came here, you basically had to live in the fields. The whole notion of town and place iden-tity changed."

I should shut up, I think. But there is a pickup truck driving on a remote county road below us.

"See that guy?" I ask. "I would imagine he knows exactly where he is. And I would also imagine he's not thinking about how this place is part of a thou-sand stories. I would imagine he has no idea the shape of that road began in Thomas Jefferson's brain. I would imagine he is not thinking about how the land he sees is evidence of a prehistoric inland sea. He does not know that we can see him and that this little Cessna's GPS can see satellites in outer space. All the stories are complicated and woven together. Why so much canola this year? Is the answer in some futures market in Chicago?"

"Sharon Parks," Tim says, "who has done a lot of writing in student affairs, has written about being on the dance floor but also needing to get up to the balcony. Both are needed. That's exactly the same idea. Both are needed. If you never dance, you never get down on the floor. If you never get to the balcony, you never see the real beauty."

"That's the blessing of altitude," I say.

"Look at this shelterbelt down here," Tim says. "It's really something."

"Take a picture."

"Ah, the thing shut off. Missed it. Missed it, sorry."

Run.

Chase.

Reach.

Large homes ring a beautiful lake south of Stump Lake. There are baseball fields behind what looks like a school. Rock piles rise out of the middle of some fields.

"The horizon is just forever today," I say.

"Oh, man."

The instruments tell me we have a headwind of 16 knots this morning at three thousand feet. I know the surface air is much calmer, but still there are ripples on the lake water.

"There is a blueness to this field!" Tim says.

"Look at that! I don't know what that is, but you're right. It's a kind of gunmetal-gray blue."

The James River is off to the left, thin and twisting. What a rush it would be, I think, to settle this airplane just a little above the river water and bank and turn my way toward Jamestown. Devil's Lake takes up the whole of the eye from in front off to the right. Two airplanes, both heading for the Devil's Lake airport and both about the same distance away, begin the dance of who gets to land first.

"The horizon gets really blue with all this water," Tim says.

Devil's Lake looks absolutely calm and beautiful on a summer morning. One airplane lands, the other announces short final, the first says he has to back-taxi, the second says he'll go around. Sorry about that, the first one says.

A thermal bumps us a little. We both smile.

Abandoned farmsteads sit in lonely and completely incongruous places. Tim and I point them out to each other. We both wonder what history put them there. What farmer or settler said, "This is the place for the barn, this is the place for the house," and then a hundred years later it clearly is not.

"This land, this farmland," Tim asks, "would be fourth generation, would you guess? From the immigrants?"

I try to do the math, but fail. How many generations ago do we count? Just back to European settlement? What about the trappers before them? What about the Métis? The Hudson Bay Company? I know a wave of New England Yankees came through before the Norwegians.

"At least," I say.

A handful of boats leave wake trails on the lake this morning. I count one, two, three, four, five—maybe more.

"Got some grain bins in the water," Tim says.

"Really? How far offshore?"

"One hundred feet. Maybe more."

Section roads, nearly white with sun-bleached gravel, run into the lake and disappear into the water. We pass over a farmstead cut neatly in two by water. The house and a couple sheds on dry land. Two large barns look like arks setting sail. We pass over Minnewaukan. Water to the north and east.

In the game of tag, there is a moment you must decide. *This* person, you think. Billy or Craig or Suzy or Anne. You've made a choice and you reach, lunge, hope. Sometimes your hand finds their head or shoulder, and you wheel hard away, laughing. Sometimes, however, you miss. Sometimes they turn in a way you did not anticipate, and your hand finds nothing but empty air. You stumble. Sometimes it's just a misstep, and you're fast back up to speed. Sometimes, however, the whole world is off balance, and you go cartwheeling through the grass, down the hill, through the brambles and thickets.

It's time to think about landing.

Sixty-nine degrees outside the airplane. Altitude: 3,000 feet. Ground speed: 89. Knots on the airspeed indicator: 97.

Ten miles away I self-announce on the radio. Straight in for Runway Three-Zero.

"I think I see what might be the runway there," I say. "It ends in the canola field."

"Ah," Tim says.

I call again at four miles out.

Tim points. "Is that it?"

"Yep, it ends in the canola field."

I pull the throttle back and set approach speeds. I call at three miles out. No one else in the pattern or on the ground in my way.

I pull the power all the way out, coasting in on a perfect glide path. Nearly silent.

Suddenly, it occurs to me that this is all wrong. I have a 14-knot headwind, and I'm about to lose it. When I do, there will be much less air moving over the wings. Less air means less lift. Less lift means I will sink, fast, right when I want to have lift the most. Without the headwind, my ground speed will also shoot up. I'll be too slow to fly and too fast to land at the very same time.

The headwind disappears just as my hand reaches to the throttle. A little power is all it takes. Increase airspeed just a bit. Our wheels hit the runway, but damn we're fast. We roll, not entirely straight, toward the canola field. I pull the throttle out and gently press the brakes.

"Sorry about that," I say.

"Can't expect everything," Tim says.

The two wind socks by the runway are empty and hanging at right angles to each other.

"You didn't want that on video, did you?" Tim asks.

"Absolutely I wanted that on video," I say. "That was without a doubt the worst landing of my entire life."

"And I was the witness!" Tim laughs. "What's the old saying? 'On a wing and a prayer'?"

"Just don't tell anyone," I say.

"Oh, there is pastoral confidentiality on this," he says.

"There is?"

"Yeah. There's stuff I just can't tell anyone!"

Tag, I think. You're it.

There is no such thing as the Geographical Center of North America. Nonetheless, we park the airplane and go inside the small terminal building. The airport has a courtesy car for pilots, and we drive through town to the Cornerstone Café. On the street side of the parking lot, a large stone cairn marks the spot. I take a picture of Tim, smiling, his hand on the rock. He takes a picture of me, smiling, arms outstretched. Even if it's all a fantasy, we are standing in a place people need to define.

The day is warm, and the sunshine is bright. There is no wind at all. We walk to the café and place an order to go. An oatmeal raisin cookie for me. A cup of coffee for Tim. Both are really very good. Back at the airport, I look at the pictures, and it dawns on me: I never touched the thing. Stood next to it, yes. But my hand did not meet the thing itself.

Tag, I think.

Or not.

Just run, chase, reach.

Short-Hop Notebook

The Swoop

It's almost like a benediction. The flight is over, nearly. You're home, or at least near an airport. You are landing. You are looking to bring the airplane to the earth and, if you are any good, kiss the pavement so gently with your tires that it's hard to know when you're down. If you fly like me, there's often a pretty good bump when wheels hit runway.

At airports without a control tower, you "self-announce" your intentions on the radio. You give your position, your altitude, the runway you are heading for. And you do this several times so other pilots in the area know where you are. If they are on the ground or near the airport, they are self-announcing too. If all goes well, we wave at each other from some distance.

At a tower-controlled airport, however, the air traffic controller keeps us all in line. The language is plain and clear, designed to avoid any misunderstanding. "Cleared to land" is the benediction, that final bit of permission every pilot enjoys hearing. Whatever challenges the landing presents—crosswinds, birds, icy concrete—are still in front of us, but the runway is all ours.

Sometimes, though, "cleared to land" is not the only instruction we hear. At a tower-controlled airport, the main job of the controller is separation, keeping us far enough away from each other that we don't make unexpected introductions. Some of the instructions require nothing more than a bit of patience. "Extend your downwind, I'll call your base" is a common instruction that allows another airplane to land in front of you. It means keep flying parallel to the runway but away from the airport until the controller tells you to turn around. You settle in, watch cars on the highways, wonder what is inside the freight trains. "Make a right/left 360" is another way to slow you down. You add a bit of power and bank the airplane into what is called a standard turn. It should take two minutes for you to get back to where you began. In the meantime, you can check out the neighborhoods near the airport. If you're still a ways out, the tower may tell you to make S turns, and you line yourself up over roads or pathways, meandering your way toward home like a kid who doesn't want to come inside. All of these instructions allow someone else to get in first. All of them allow for a bit more flying.

Sometimes, though, the instruction is to hurry up. And, to be honest, this is fun. "Make short approach" is the phrase that means the tower is hoping to get you in before someone else. It means cut power, add carb heat if you have it, put in first flaps, push the yoke forward, and bank. You do *not* want to use the rudder to sharpen the turn. You still have to correct for crosswinds. As you bring in more flaps, you still have to be aware of the potential for an accelerated stall. But this is movie flying. This is the swoop, the barnstormer coming over the barn and banking hard before the silo. This is the fighter coming in to land at the aircraft carrier. Instead of the long approach that looks more like a factory production line than art, this is old-time flying. Inside the airplane, this is what we imagined when we were five years old. This is what we imagined it must be like.

A lot of pilots call this a cowboy landing. And this is just so damn pretty it makes you smile.

That Thing Up Front

Here is a truth about my flying history. My first flight lesson never happened. The instructor, a man way too tall to fit into the ancient and glorious 152 we were about to use, walked me out to the airplane and began to talk about the preflight inspection. I checked the fuel and the oil. I checked the ailerons and flaps, the air pressure in the tires, and the amount of travel in the front strut. I was ready to fly.

When I got to the prop, I ran my hand down the length of each blade. I remember feeling the subtle twist in the shape. And I remember the way the blade curved back at the end, like a winglet.

"Wait," my instructor said. "That's not what it should be."

A mechanic was called. He frowned; then we all frowned. Someone had run something into the end of the propeller. It would have to be removed and fixed. "That propeller," he said, "would shake the engine right out of the plane." Unhappy, but safe, we all went back inside. Yet there is something about the feel of that shape in my hand I have never forgotten. Even now, when I preflight an airplane, I begin at the nose, with my hand running the length and curve of a propeller. If there is magic in an airplane, I think, it resides in the prop.

Archimedes, the mathematician from ancient Greece, is generally credited with inventing the first propeller-like tool—the screw. And while the screw may not look very much like an airplane prop, the basic principle is the same. What's changed are just the math and the materials.

Jeremy Kinney, curator for aircraft propulsion at the Smithsonian National Air and Space Museum, oversees aircraft propulsion in general, and in particular aerial propeller development. "Propellers have their own story," he says, "and it's just as dynamic as you can imagine." There are 527 propellers in the museum, many of them representing new ideas in design or materials. Walk in the main entrance on Independence Avenue, and one of the first things you see is the *Rutan Voyager,* the first plane to circumnavigate the globe without stopping or refueling, and the Hartzell constant-speed props crucial to its long-distance performance. A prop from the *Enola Gay* is here. Whereas the prop from the original *Wright Flyer* is in a case near the *Flyer* (the airplane was overturned on the ground in a gust of wind, and the prop was damaged), the *Spirit of St. Louis* boasts its original propeller. "Lindbergh insisted on a metal propeller," says Kinney. "His was the first well-known use of the ground adjustable-pitch idea."

I ask him what are some of the most significant props in the collection. "Our newest prop—the Dowty R391—is from a C-130 transport," he said. "Six blades. Composite. Hydraulically actuated. It really is the latest, most up-to-date prop there is. But to me, the most important propellers are the Hamilton Standard props of the 1920s, '30s, and '40s. These became the standard, especially the Hydromatic constant-speed propeller. Every DC-3 had these Hydromatic props. Every B-17. Just about every Allied airplane had Hydromatic props. They are the basic core of what all modern propellers are."

To be accurate, a propeller is a rotating wing in a helical path. Because it's a wing, pitch and angle of attack are the problems that keep engineers awake at night. The Wright brothers introduced the twist in the blade, but every inch of a blade should be maximally efficient. Remember calculus class? Change one variable, such as the engine or airframe behind the prop, and you have a whole new set of efficiency goals.

At Sensenich, Steve Boser, vice president, says, "We make somewhere between seventy-five and a hundred fixed-pitch propeller models. About twenty-five of those are what you could call our most popular. Well over one hundred different airplane models fly with our props." Sensenich divides its products roughly into 50 percent aircraft, 35 percent airboat, and 15 percent UAV for the military.

"We also service the antique market," he says. "A lot of our wooden props are made to order. J-3 props are popular, as are Stearman, Fairchild, Stinson props. There are some really obscure ones, too, like the Funk B or Bird BK. Every one of them has different needs. We even make the test clubs for overhaul shops, something to put a load on an engine that's being overhauled.

"It's a continuing evolution of engineering," Boser says. "New materials such as composites allow new shapes. New engines or airframes demand new shapes. New ways of computing data make design efficiencies easier. We're able to push the boundaries with new materials."

Small differences are everything in the propeller world. The difference between a climb prop and a cruise prop is only a small difference in pitch. The difference between a land and a sea prop is only pitch, and sometimes diameter, since the airplane sits higher off the ground. But in those small differences is a universe of theory and testing and math. What engineers call the "slowdown effect" describes how fuselage airflow affects prop performance. "Scrubbing drag" or "nonuniform inflow distribution" talks about how the air reaching the base of the prop is moving slower than the "freestream velocity" at the tip, which can have a dramatic effect on the loading.

Scott Hickman, product support manager at McCauley Propellers, says the company produces thousands of constant-speed and fixed-pitch configurations for commercial, military, UAV, and general aviation. Because McCauley's parent company is Cessna, every propeller-driven Cessna airplane is delivered with a McCauley prop. "We've had significant advances in design and testing software," he says. "It's all about efficiency, but also about reducing noise and vibration."

In 1941 McCauley produced the first forged ground-adjustable steel propeller, and they went on to produce more than twenty thousand of them during World War II. In 1970 they introduced their first threadless-blade retention system. In 2010 they introduced their first significant production of a composite fixed-pitch propeller for the Cessna 162 Skycatcher. "We're in the certification phase of introducing a composite constant-speed prop," Hickman says. "We use the VARTM method, which means vacuum-assisted resin-transfer molding process. There's no erosion on these blades. A lot better longevity."

In Dayton, Ohio, a man named Robert Hartzell lived down the street from a man named Orville Wright. Whereas the first propellers on the Wright brothers' airplanes were made by the brothers, Orville convinced Robert to take over the manufacturing in 1917. Today, Hartzell Propeller makes about three hundred different blade designs that go into about twelve hundred propeller models. They make only constant-speed props and limit their upper end to engines under 1800 horsepower.

According to Mike Disbrow, senior vice president for marketing and customer services, Hartzell props have some interesting distinctions. A Hartzell prop is on the *Rutan Voyager*. A Hartzell prop helped set the altitude record for a piston airplane. Like everyone else, though, the engineers at Hartzell think about efficiency, noise, and weight. Their Q-tip prop, with the tip bent back like the one that kept me grounded, used on Twin Commanders, uses what amounts to an upside-down winglet at the prop end to reduce noise while keeping thrust numbers up. "We use ASC-II," Disbrow says. "Advanced structural composite, version two. Carbon. Kevlar. Fully composite instead of a metal spar or wooden core. Our first composites were developed for the regional airlines—the lower weight meant greater payload. Now we've refined that process into a better version two."

Their scimitar prop is a new release. It really does look like a classical Middle Eastern sword blade. "There are two reasons for that shape," says Disbrow. "The first is noise. There is some real noise reduction in that tip shape. The second is aesthetic. It's just a really pretty propeller."

It's a sad fact that the first passenger death in a powered aircraft was caused by propeller failure. Orville Wright was the pilot, and Lieutenant Thomas Selfridge was along on an inspection ride for the army. One hundred and fifty feet above the ground, the right propeller came apart, sliced a wire, and destroyed the rudder. The airplane glided to about seventy-five feet AGL, then went nose first into the ground. Wright was severely injured. Selfridge never regained consciousness and died at the hospital.

However, according to David Kenny, accident statistician at the Aircraft Owners and Pilots Association (AOPA) Air Safety Institute, fixed-wing accidents caused by structural or mechanical failures of either fixed-pitch or constant-speed propellers are rare. There were 99 during the ten years from 2001 through 2010 inclusive, 14 of which were fatal. This represents seven-tenths of 1 percent (0.7 percent) of the 14,120 light fixed-wing GA accidents during the same period and half of 1 percent (0.5 percent) of all fatal accidents. Half of them (49 of 99, including 6 of the 14 fatals) occurred in amateur-built aircraft. Blade and hub failures accounted for 31 of the amateur-built accidents, 1 was caused by undertorqued prop bolts, and 10 were due to failures of drive belts or reduction-gear assemblies. The remaining 7 were failures in pitch-change mechanisms in constant-speed props. Among manufactured airplanes, blade and hub failures caused 29 of 50, undertorqued bolts caused 3, and pitch-change mechanisms caused 10. The remaining 8 were due to leaks in oil lines or the constant-speed hub itself.

There are a thousand ways to imagine a propeller. Few things are more complicated. Few things are more simple. It's a rotating wing in a helical path. On the 172 I rent, it's forty-two pounds. To Hollywood, it's adventure and romance and thrill. To an engineer, it's a history of physics, materials, and math.

$$C_P = \frac{0.0005 \times BHP}{\sigma \times \left(\frac{N}{1000}\right)^3 \times \left(\frac{D}{10}\right)^5}$$

Finally, though, it's a smooth shape in a pilot's hand on a clear morning when all we want is the sky itself. It's the thing up front that makes us go.

A Very Deep Low

One of the strongest storms in the history of the central U.S. affected the region on October 26-27, 2010, producing wind gusts over 50 mph across much of the Midwest, severe thunderstorms and tornadoes from southeast Wisconsin and northeast Illinois to northern Alabama, and a blizzard over northern Minnesota and North Dakota. As the storm reached peak intensity late during the afternoon on October 26 over Minnesota, the lowest barometric pressure readings ever recorded in the central United States occurred. A reading of 28.21 (955.2 mb [millibars]) was recorded at Bigfork, MN, a pressure that is found in Category 3 hurricanes!

—National Oceanic and Atmospheric Administration
(NOAA), National Weather Service website, "The
October 26-27, 2010, Record Extratropical Cyclone"

It seems to be a law of nature. Leave the country, go to someplace known for its very bad weather—hell, go there *because* of the bad weather—and your days there will be sunny and fine, while back home the sky will rent and tear and the winds will blow and all sorts of trouble will come unglued.

So I admit I was gone for this one. I was in Scotland, hiking the West Highland Way with students. It rained, but not very hard. The wind blew, but not very fast. The trail was solid, and the pubs were warm. It was a wonderful trip. And then the alerts started coming. Watches and warnings from the Weather Service in Grand Forks. E-mail from family and friends. *Do you know what you're missing? We have a hurricane on the prairie!*

To illustrate how strong of a storm this is, 28.21 inches is equivalent to a Category 3 Hurricane. The lowest pressure for the storm that sank the "Edmund Fitzgerald" on November 10, 1975 was 28.95 inches. Even with the Armistice Day storm, the lowest pressure recorded was 28.55 inches. Of course, pressure is only one measurement of a storm.

—Minnesota Climatology Working Group website

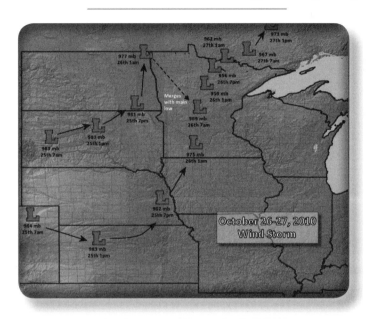

When you miss a storm, you look for the people who were there. You look for the people who paid attention, who you can trust to get it right, who know the value of a detail. Daryl Ritchison is the morning meteorologist for WDAY television and radio in Fargo, North Dakota, and a friend. Tall and skinny with an infectious smile, he's every bit the community star that weather people tend to be. He's also the real thing. He knows his science.

"Daryl," I said on the phone. "I wasn't here. I need to know what happened. Can I come over?"

A few days later, I'm sitting in the television studio, in the weather section of the news set. A dozen television and computer monitors bring real-time data to the glow.

"I leave the country, and this big hairy storm happens," I say. "Everyone on e-mail is writing. Seventy-mile-an-hour winds. Eighty-mile-an-hour winds. Lows stronger than most hurricanes. You have no idea what you're missing!"

Daryl smiles at me as his telephone rings. A few months ago, he and his wife appeared in a local version of *Dancing with the Stars*. The woman on the phone is asking him to be a part of a *Singing with the Stars* event. Daryl confesses he can't sing a note, but this is a fund-raiser, so he's game.

"Daryl, what happened?" I ask when he hangs up.

"The storm," he says, "in some ways, you know, did move into the area, and then in other ways it formed over us. The animation I sent you, and a lot of the animations, will take you through about twenty-four hours, but that twenty-four hours is actually when the storm 'bombed'—bombogenesis. The action occurred over the state of Minnesota, but this was a piece of energy that did move in from the Pacific Ocean, moved across the Rockies, and then bombed out over the Upper Midwest."

"Wait," I say. "Bombogenesis?"

"A low-pressure system, outside the tropics, where the pressure falls at least twenty-four millibars in twenty-four hours."

"That's a lot," I say.

"*Bomb* is a very good word," Daryl says. "So this storm, it may have had the lowest atmospheric pressure observed in the United States. There have been areas of low pressure in Alaska far lower than this. And there've been areas of low pressure off the West Coast that, because they didn't hit a buoy correctly, didn't generate the right data, which were probably lower as well. Yet this storm set the record. And at that level, it's impressive. But you know what? It did not create the highest wind speeds ever. It's hard to tell people this, but we've had more impressive windstorms than this one. This area of low pressure was very deep, but the gradient associated with it wasn't as strong as, say, the storm in 1998, because there was no high-pressure system that differentiated the low behind it. This wind was almost 100 percent just created from the intensity of the low. We get better pressure gradients and higher wind speeds from a weaker low with a high situated right on its shoulder."

"What were the winds?" I ask.

"The airport peaked out at sixty-four. But Hector Field has a sonic wind gauge, sound waves do it, and sometimes it goes a little quirky. I will never deny the sixty-four-mile-an-hour wind speed, but at other airports, most of the wind speeds were more fifty to fifty-five."

METAR KFAR 262253Z 28035G50KT 4SM RA BR OVC019 03/01 A2859

URGENT—WINTER WEATHER MESSAGE
NATIONAL WEATHER SERVICE GRAND FORKS ND
310 PM CDT MON OCT 25 2010
. . . THE FIRST WINTER STORM OF THE SEASON IS POSSIBLE TUESDAY NIGHT AND WEDNESDAY . . .
A STRONG AREA OF LOW PRESSURE WILL BRING A VARIETY OF

WEATHER TO THE ENTIRE REGION. RAIN IS EXPECTED TO CHANGE TO SNOW IN THE DEVILS LAKE BASIN LATE TUESDAY AFTERNOON . . . WITH THE CHANGE OVER OCCURRING TUESDAY NIGHT IN THE RED RIVER VALLEY. STRONG WINDS GUSTING OVER 50 MPH COULD COMBINE WITH THE SNOW TO PRODUCE LOW VISIBILITIES TUES-DAY NIGHT AND WEDNESDAY . . . WITH NEAR BLIZZARD CONDI-TIONS POSSIBLE FOR THE WEDNESDAY MORNING COMMUTE.

. . . WINTER STORM WATCH IN EFFECT FROM LATE TUESDAY NIGHT THROUGH WEDNESDAY EVENING . . .

THE NATIONAL WEATHER SERVICE IN GRAND FORKS HAS IS-SUED A WINTER STORM WATCH . . . WHICH IS IN EFFECT FROM LATE TUESDAY NIGHT THROUGH WEDNESDAY EVENING.

* RAIN WILL CHANGE TO SNOW LATE TUESDAY AFTERNOON IN THE DEVILS LAKE BASIN. THE CHANGE OVER TO SNOW WILL OC-CUR BY LATE TUESDAY NIGHT IN THE RED RIVER VALLEY. SNOW MAY BECOME HEAVY AT TIMES LATE TUESDAY NIGHT INTO WEDNESDAY MORNING.

* SNOW ACCUMULATIONS OF 6 INCHES OR MORE ARE POSSIBLE IN THE DEVILS LAKE BASIN INTO NORTHEAST NORTH DAKOTA. ACCUMULATIONS MAY VARY GREATLY OVER SHORT DISTANCES DUE TO THE BANDED NATURE OF HEAVIER SNOW.

* WEST TO NORTHWEST WINDS WILL GUST OVER 50 MPH AT TIMES TUESDAY NIGHT INTO WEDNESDAY. THIS COULD CAUSE NEAR BLIZZARD CONDITIONS NEAR HEAVIER SNOW BANDS . . . AND VISIBILITIES MAY FALL BELOW ONE QUARTER OF A MILE AT TIMES IN OPEN AREAS.

* ROADS MAY BECOME SNOW COVERED AND SLICK FOR THE WEDNESDAY MORNING COMMUTE.

PRECAUTIONARY/PREPAREDNESS ACTIONS . . .

A WINTER STORM WATCH MEANS THERE IS A POTENTIAL FOR SIGNIFICANT SNOW . . . SLEET . . . OR ICE ACCUMULATIONS THAT MAY IMPACT TRAVEL.

CONTINUE TO MONITOR THE LATEST FORECASTS.

"The 1888 Children's Blizzard was under 29.5," I say.

"Perhaps," Daryl replies. "I wouldn't trust it because there were no sensors. It could've been much, much lower."

"But they had military personnel doing barometer readings."

"Those were primitive, and few and far between. This storm, again, had it not been for stations added in the past decade, would not have broken a re-cord. You need something that is calibrated and official to break it."

"Armistice Day was 28.55."

Daryl smiles.

"Katrina was 27.22. Andrew was 27.23."

"And this prairie storm bottomed out at 28.21."

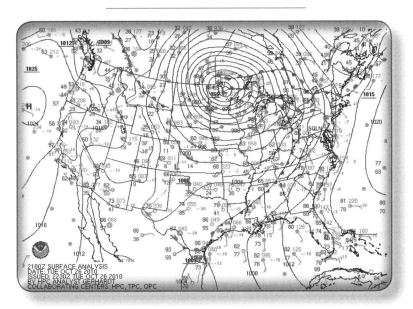

URGENT—WEATHER MESSAGE

NATIONAL WEATHER SERVICE GRAND FORKS ND

1018 AM CDT MON OCT 25 2010

. . . STRONG WINDS WILL MOVE INTO THE AREA LATE TONIGHT AND TUESDAY . . .

NORTHWEST WINDS WILL INCREASE LATE TONIGHT AND GUST OVER 50 MPH BY TUESDAY AFTERNOON THROUGHOUT THE RED RIVER VALLEY. IN ADDITION . . . RAIN WILL CHANGE TO SNOW LATE TUESDAY NIGHT AND WEDNESDAY MORNING . . . AND DANGEROUS WINTER WEATHER CONDITIONS MAY DEVELOP. STAY TUNED TO LATER STATEMENTS ON THIS POWERFUL STORM SYSTEM THAT WILL AFFECT THE REGION THROUGH WEDNESDAY.

. . . HIGH WIND WATCH IN EFFECT FROM TUESDAY MORNING THROUGH LATE TUESDAY NIGHT . . .

THE NATIONAL WEATHER SERVICE IN GRAND FORKS HAS ISSUED A HIGH WIND WATCH . . . WHICH IS IN EFFECT FROM TUESDAY MORNING THROUGH LATE TUESDAY NIGHT.

＊STRONG NORTHWEST WINDS FROM 35 TO 45 MPH . . . WITH GUSTS OVER 55 MPH WILL DEVELOP LATE TONIGHT AND CONTINUE

INTO WEDNESDAY. IN ADDITION . . . COLDER AIR WILL FILTER INTO THE REGION TUESDAY NIGHT AND CHANGE RAIN TO SNOW.

* ACCUMULATING SNOW IS ALSO POSSIBLE TUESDAY NIGHT AND WEDNESDAY IN THE DEVILS LAKE BASIN INTO THE RED RIVER VALLEY. THE SNOW IN COMBINATION WITH THE STRONG WINDS MAY PRODUCE REDUCED VISIBILITIES AND DANGEROUS TRAVEL CONDITIONS LATE TUESDAY NIGHT INTO WEDNESDAY.

PRECAUTIONARY/PREPAREDNESS ACTIONS . . .

A HIGH WIND WATCH MEANS THERE IS THE POTENTIAL FOR A HAZARDOUS HIGH WIND EVENT. SUSTAINED WINDS OF AT LEAST 40 MPH . . . OR GUSTS OF 58 MPH OR STRONGER MAY OCCUR. CONTINUE TO MONITOR THE LATEST FORECASTS.

"Tell me this," I say. "*Why* did this storm happen?"

A technician reminds Daryl he has a radio spot coming up.

"You ready?" he asks me.

I nod.

"There was a supertyphoon called Magi. It was the strongest tropical system on the planet so far this year. It impacted the Philippines in the middle of October. At the same time, there was this whole oscillation pattern called the Madden Julian Oscillation. It's this oscillation pattern that oftentimes starts in the Indian Ocean, moves through Indonesia, west to east, and then goes out in the Pacific. It gradually gets over cooler water, dies, and then the oscillation pattern starts all over. It takes energy away from the atmosphere, if you want to look at it that way, and probably lowers sea-surface temperatures a little bit, so there's not quite as much energy there.

"So this is anywhere from a thirty- to sixty-day oscillation pattern. I pay attention to it because it can impact us here in the Midwest. What was going on in October was we had this oscillation, and when it comes through, think of it as a cluster of thunderstorms, a big mass of moisture energy working its way through the Indian Ocean out in the Pacific. It was not related to the typhoon. The typhoon was forming separately in the western Pacific. This oscillation pattern happened to get into the western Pacific. At approximately the same time, we had the largest tropical system of the year. The Madden Julian Oscillation was coming, so we have these two pockets of massive energy that somewhat combined. We have a very strong La Niña that has developed and is enhancing the jet stream over the Pacific. To get an area of low pressure, you have to have good lift. That's what's lowering the pressure, to put it simply. This pocket of energy happened to get picked up from a jet stream enhanced slightly from La Niña, so we have this huge amount of energy, and we already had a storm in place, a trough over the United States, and it all came together, and poof! We get this intense area of low pressure bombing out over the Midwest.

"Now we've had storms. This storm I would probably rank way down low in the thousands for impressiveness of actual impacts. We've had more storms than a human could count that had greater human impacts. Stronger winds, heavier rains, heavier snow, right through the list. More damage from severe weather. But this one has no competition when it comes to atmospheric pressure, from what we know. It broke that particular record. But that's all it was. Just low pressure. That's all it was. The storm was impressive for its wind field and pressure, not for huge human impacts."

"Looking at the animation," I say, "I would swear there was an eye to that thing."

"Oftentimes you get little ones from latitude cyclones like this. So it wouldn't surprise me if there was a little something there."

URGENT—WEATHER MESSAGE
NATIONAL WEATHER SERVICE GRAND FORKS ND
258 PM CDT MON OCT 25 2010
. . . VERY STRONG WINDS EXPECTED TUESDAY . . .
A VERY STRONG STORM SYSTEM WILL BE CENTERED OVER NORTHERN MINNESOTA TUESDAY AFTERNOON AND IS EXPECTED TO RESULT IN VERY STRONG WINDS ACROSS THE NORTHERN PLAINS. NORTHWEST WINDS WILL BEGIN TO INCREASE LATE TONIGHT WITH GUSTS UP TO 60 MPH POSSIBLE ACROSS THE

DEVILS LAKE REGION . . . SOUTHERN RED RIVER VALLEY . . . AND
WEST CENTRAL MINNESOTA BY TUESDAY AFTERNOON. THE
WINDS SHOULD ALSO BE STRONG ACROSS THE NORTHERN VAL-
LEY AND NORTHWEST MINNESOTA . . . BUT THERE IS STILL SOME
QUESTION AS TO THE POTENTIAL FOR GUSTS APPROACHING 60
MPH. THE STRONG WESTERLY AND NORTHWESTERLY WINDS WILL
CONTINUE THROUGH TUESDAY EVENING WITH RAIN DURING
THE AFTERNOON AND GRADUALLY CHANGING OVER TO SNOW
TUESDAY EVENING.

. . . HIGH WIND WARNING IN EFFECT FROM 1 PM TUESDAY TO 1
AM CDT WEDNESDAY . . .

THE NATIONAL WEATHER SERVICE IN GRAND FORKS HAS IS-
SUED A HIGH WIND WARNING . . . WHICH IS IN EFFECT FROM 1 PM
TUESDAY TO 1 AM CDT WEDNESDAY. THE HIGH WIND WATCH IS
NO LONGER IN EFFECT.

* STRONG NORTHWEST WINDS FROM 35 TO 45 MPH . . . WITH
GUSTS UP TO 60 MPH WILL DEVELOP BY TUESDAY AFTERNOON
THROUGH TUESDAY EVENING. STRONG WINDS WILL CONTINUE
THROUGH TUESDAY NIGHT INTO WEDNESDAY.

* HAZARDOUS CONDITIONS ARE EXPECTED ON DEVILS LAKE
DUE TO WAVE HEIGHTS OF 5 TO 7 FEET . . . WITH THE HIGHEST
WAVES ON THE EASTERN SHORES OF THE LAKE.

* THE STORM SYSTEM WILL USHER IN COLDER AIR INTO THE RE-
GION TUESDAY AFTERNOON AND TUESDAY EVENING . . . CHANG-
ING ANY RAIN TO SNOW TUESDAY EVENING. THE COMBINATION
OF THE HIGH WINDS AND FALLING SNOW IN THE DEVILS LAKE
REGION MAY CREATE HAZARDOUS TRAVEL CONDITIONS DUE TO
BLOWING SNOW.

PRECAUTIONARY/PREPAREDNESS ACTIONS . . .

A HIGH WIND WARNING MEANS A HAZARDOUS HIGH WIND
EVENT IS EXPECTED OR OCCURRING. SUSTAINED WIND SPEEDS
OF AT LEAST 40 MPH OR GUSTS OF 58 MPH OR MORE CAN LEAD TO
PROPERTY DAMAGE.

"How many days do we have wind gusts of forty-seven, forty-three, forty-
nine?" Daryl asks. "All the time! This just kinda stepped a little bit over the
line again. It's much harder to impress a meteorologist in these things. But it
was very entertaining; it was very fun. I always tell people that we get down
30, 35 below most winters. Most summers we're flirting with 100, if we don't
hit 100. With this wet cycle, the ground is a little more saturated, so our 102s
have turned into 97s, but it's really the same thing. So we have this 130- to

140-degree temperature swing every year, and *that's not unusual here!* But only the core of North America and in some ways the core of Siberia get this extreme weather. In Seattle their lowest all winter might be 10 to 20 degrees, and they may hit 90 once or twice. They have a 70-degree range all year. We can do that in a week. We've almost done that in a day. That's why I love living here. We have more of a temperature extreme than most of the population on earth experiences ever. We take it for granted because we see it so often. Then add in thunderstorms and blizzards and tornadoes and heat waves. So it's all very cool."

In strong wind, sailors reef and furl their sails. In very strong wind, they may go "bare poles," no sails at all, just the wind against the hull and rigging and a prayer at the wheel.

In strong wind, pilots stay on the ground.

October 26, 2010. No flight lessons. No charter flights. At 12:30 p.m. a request for the fixed-wing air ambulance comes in and is turned down due to weather. At 4:45 another request comes in, turned down due to weather. At 7:40 a request comes in for the helicopter ambulance, turned down due to weather. A DC-9 makes two attempts to land on Runway 27 and then decides to return to Minneapolis. United Airlines cancels six flights. American Airlines cancels two.

October 27. The airport in Minneapolis closes all but one runway because of high winds. In Fargo, United Airlines cancels eight flights. American cancels one.

Daryl and I say good-bye, and I walk outside into a bright, sunny, calm, and warm November day. What small clouds there are seem drawn for a children's book. If I didn't know any better, I think to myself. We've already had hard snow in western North Dakota. The season is changing. Pretty soon we'll have blizzards. Deep low pressure will bring storms. High pressure will bring clear skies and lethal cold. I have been here for all of this. If I didn't know any better, I think, I wouldn't know any better.

I'm sorry I missed the storm.

Monster Sky

From the air, you can hardly see the change.

White snow on every field. White snow to every horizon. Dark, meandering ribbons of riparian trees intersect beige lines of gravel roads, section roads, as straight as an assayer's dream. Ice on every river, every lake, every pond. A calendar picture of winter.

But this is the middle of March, and the colors have changed. River ice, no longer hard and perfect white, morphs into yellow and gray, the snow and ice starting to merge with the water below. Field snow melts and then refreezes as ice, reflecting blue sky less brilliantly, more like a mirror. Trees and buildings grow a darker brown. In neighborhoods, streaks of black reveal where snow has melted in alleys and backyards. Plow-built walls on the boulevards are dirty gray, the sand and gravel coming together as the snow and ice melt, exactly the same process that built every glacial moraine. In miniature there are icefalls and *bergschrunds* and seracs at every bend in the river.

If you look closely, you can see something happening. Not just here or there. The whole landscape changing, the end of winter on the northern prairie. Blizzards and lethal cold are still possible, even expected. But as I walk around the airplane, the preflight inspection, I step over puddles of meltwater. I fold my jacket into the backseat. In April and May I would smile at this weather and declare it a fine and lovely day. The sky is bright and clear and warm. Yet here is a strange thing about living on the northern prairie. Too warm, too early, is the start of disaster.

One thousand feet above the North Dakota farmland, it's possible to see the world shimmer and tremble in the sunlight. Words like *alpenglow* and *pearlescent* would work this afternoon. The Red River is still frozen, as is the Sheyenne. The sky is bright blue and the sunshine enormous. The fields are still snow covered, but the ice is compressing and melting away from the bottom. It's all the same. It's all completely different. From the air, city streets seem fluid as cars and trucks splash through curbside puddles that reach out toward medians and centerlines.

The world is becoming fat, I think. Swelling. Like the bottom of Lake Yellowstone. Like the side of Mount Saint Helens.

Just a few days ago, in Japan, an earthquake now measured at 9.0 moved the coastline eight feet. Tens of thousands of people are dead or missing. Tsunamis, rising as high as one hundred feet in harbors and bays, rushed ashore and then pulled the unattached and the unready back out to sea. Nuclear reactors are burning and venting radiation. The earth has shifted four inches on its axis.

Just a few weeks ago, a New Zealand earthquake measured 6.3, killed at least 166, and brought down the spire at the Canterbury Cathedral in Christchurch, where just a few months ago I lit a candle and then climbed the stairs to see the city at sunset.

Just last weekend, a Dakota blizzard came down so hard it stranded hundreds on the highways.

New Jersey is flooding. Tennessee is flooding. At North Dakota's Baldhill Dam, just a few hours ago, the drawdown of Lake Ashtabula was finished, and the valves were closed enough to match outflow with inflow. We all know what's coming.

I turn the airplane north and then west, following country roads and the paths of creeks whose names I have not learned. It's a beautiful day. The sky is everywhere and bright. Enveloping. There has to be a word, I think, a word that gets to the heart of this feeling and this sight. *Beautiful* and *apprehensive* come to mind and then fade away. Both words are too easy, too gentle, too soft. There needs to be something more about the size of this air. The weight of that size. The potential of the enormous.

Then it comes to me. *Monster*. I am flying in a *monster* sky. Huge and complicated. As likely to love as to kill.

Spring in North Dakota, especially in the eastern part of the state, can often disappoint. The Sun climbs higher in the sky each day, but the winter snow cover and a persistent wind from Canada often make spring a dream that never seems to come true. When the snow finally melts and you find out that the rumors are true, that indeed, there is still grass under the snow, more snow falls and once again the landscape turns into a sea of white. It is a season when your entire wardrobe is needed, from shorts and t-shirts, to winter jackets and scarves and sometimes, you may use all of those items in a single day. True spring, flowers blooming, with green grass as lush and soft as your bed with yourself relaxing on the patio reading a good book under a warm refreshing sun will come eventually. Perhaps this season instead of being called spring, should instead be referred to as patience, as most years we need plenty of it.

    —E-mail from Daryl Ritchison, meteorologist, WDAY, Fargo, North Dakota

How do you describe the invisible? Better yet, how do you measure a feeling?

Insolation is the term the scientists use to measure how much energy from the sun is hitting a spot on the earth. It's measured in kilowatt hours per square meter of planet. Length of day and angle of the sun are the main variables, and in the Northern Hemisphere springtime means longer days and higher angle, more energy from the sun reaching each field of snow and ice. So somewhere, I think, there has to be a chart or a table or a graph that tells me how much insolation the prairie receives. The numbers are important. How much more in March than in February? How much more in July than December?

The headline doesn't really surprise anyone—

TROOPERS: 800 MOTORISTS RESCUED AFTER ND BLIZZARD
By JAMES MacPHERSON
updated 3/12/2011 2:33:52 PM ET BISMARCK, N.D.—Rescue workers used military trucks and other heavy vehicles to pluck motorists from more than 500 vehicles abandoned along ice-slicked roads and in drifting snow throughout North Dakota and take them to churches, schools, bars and gas stations that became makeshift shelters.

About 800 people were rescued starting Friday afternoon, and most remained at shelters Saturday as highways remained closed. North Dakota National Guard spokesman Capt. Dan Murphy said the rescue mission ended Saturday morning but soldiers were still on duty, patrolling highway entrances.

Only minor injuries had been reported following hundreds of pileups and crashes, Highway Patrol Lt. Jody Skogen said. A no travel advisory had been lifted, but snow and abandoned cars still blocked the roads, authorities said.

Winds of more than 60 mph created whiteouts during Friday's blizzard. North Dakota State College freshman Katie Woodbury was driving from the school in Fargo to her family's farm in Stanley, in northwest North Dakota, when road conditions forced her to take shelter at a church in Medina.

"It was scary—I was talking to myself the whole time," she said of her drive. "I just want to get home and see my mom and dad and the 13 new piglets at the farm." . . .

About 70 soldiers took part in the rescues, using military trucks that could plow through huge snow drifts to collect scores of stranded drivers and take them "to any warm building that was available," Murphy said. . . .

Jim Albrecht, the emergency manager in Stutsman County, said about 600 people were still taking shelter in Medina and other small towns there. He said he couldn't remember a worse storm in a state known for nasty winter weather. The storm created a white-out from the get-go, and people became stuck immediately.

"It's been a long time since we had a storm like this that hit us so hard and so fast," he said.

—http://www.msnbc.msn.com/id/42049130/ns/weather/?GT1=43001

One thing that I find interesting about the change of seasons, especially at the equinoxes, is the lag that mother nature experiences during the transition. On the equinoxes all locations on earth experience equal amounts of daylight and night. Living in the Northern Plains of the United States, the conditions on the autumnal equinox and the vernal equinox are significantly different. From a climatological perspective, the average high temperature on the autumnal equinox is 66 degrees Fahrenheit and the average high temperature on the vernal equinox is 37 degrees Fahrenheit for Grand Forks. The first inch of snow can be expected to remain on the ground during the first week of November and the last inch of snow melts during the first week of April. It almost seems unfair in March that astronomical spring arrives before climatological spring after a brutal Northern Plains winter, but the waning days of summer are almost taken for granted in September.

—E-mail from Professor Fred Remer, Department
of Atmospheric Sciences, University of North Dakota

I find what I am looking for. But I have no idea what this means—

SOLAR RADIATION ENTERING THE EARTH SYSTEM

In order to study the effects of solar radiation on the Earth system, it is necessary to determine the amount of energy reaching the Earth's atmosphere & surface. Once the surface irradiance of the Sun is determined the amount of energy reaching the top of the Earth's atmosphere can be calculated using the Inverse Square Law. The average amount of energy received on a surface perpendicular to incoming radiation at the top of the atmosphere is the solar constant. (*While this calculation can lead to a better student understanding of the Inverse Square Law, the accepted value is a yearly average from NASA satellite measurements.*)

Solar Radiation Striking the top of the Earth's Atmosphere

The Inverse Square Law is used to calculate the decrease in radiation intensity due to an increase in distance from the radiation source.

Inverse Square Law: $I = E(4\pi \times R^2)/(4\pi \times r^2)$

I = Irradiance at the surface of the outer sphere
E = Irradiance at the surface of the object (Sun)
$4\pi \times R^2$ = surface area of the object
$4\pi \times r^2$ = surface area of the outer sphere

In order to calculate the solar constant the following equation is used:

So = E(Sun) x (R(Sun) / r)²
So = Solar Constant
E = Surface Irradiance of the Sun
R = 6.96 x 10⁵ km = Radius of the Sun
r = 1.5 x 10⁸ km = Average Sun-Earth Distance

Insolation: Solar Radiation Striking the Surface

I = S cos Z
I = Insolation
S~ 1000 W/m² (*Clear day solar insolation on a surface perpendicular to incoming solar radiation. This value actually varies greatly due to atmospheric variables.*)
Z = Zenith Angle (*Zenith Angle is the angle from the zenith (point directly overhead) to the Sun's position in the sky. The zenith angle is dependent upon latitude, solar declination angle, and time of day.*)

$Z = \cos^{-1}(\sin\Phi \sin\delta + \cos\Phi \cos\delta \cos H)$

Φ = Latitude
H = = Hour Angle = 15° x (Time—12) (*Angle of radiation due to time of day. Time is given in solar time as the hour of the day from midnight.*)

δ = Solar Declination Angle

Solar Declination Angles for the Northern Hemisphere
Vernal Equinox Mar. 21/22 δ = 0°
Summer Solstice Jun. 21/22 δ = +23.5°
Autumnal Equinox Sept. 21/22 δ = 0°
Winter Solstice Dec. 21/22 δ = -23.5°

—http://edmall.gsfc.nasa.gov/inv99Project.Site/
Pages/science-briefs/ed-stickler/ed-irradiance.html

I look up the meaning of *monster* in the *Oxford English Dictionary.* I find this—

†2. Something extraordinary or unnatural; an amazing event or occurrence; a prodigy, a marvel. *Obs.*

c1384 *Bible (Wycliffite, E.V.)* (Douce 369(2)) (1850) 2 Macc. v. 4 Alle men preyeden, the monstris [L. *monstra*] or wondres, . . . for to be togidre turned in to good.

But I also find this—

c. *Math.* The largest known sporadic finite simple group (see quot. *1998*). More fully monster group, monster simple group. The group represents the symmetries of a 196,883-dimensional geometrical object, and also of a particular variety of string theory.

If you live on the prairie, "symmetry" is deep-gut home stuff. You see it in every field, in the *V* of goose flocks, in the bright spots and rings of winter sun dogs. And if you live on the prairie, especially the tallgrass flatland prairie, the notion of anything having 196,883 dimensions is alluring and a little bit dangerous—like the sound of a saxophone playing solo blues on a street corner late at night. So I write a colleague to help me understand.

Scott—
I don't know if I can manage to explain in "a few" words, but I'll try to give an answer that is understandable. In this email, I'll give the mathematical explanation. Later today or tomorrow I'll try to write you an email with a few more philosophical musings on the place of the monster in logic and human thought.
1. (Symmetries) Different objects are symmetric in different ways. A symmetry is a way to move the object, so that it looks exactly the same afterwards as it did before. For example, the letter T could be flipped over a vertical line running down the middle, and you would never know the difference. The letter X has that symmetry too, but it could also be flipped horizontally and look the same—so it has more symmetries than T does. The letter N can't be flipped without looking different, but you could rotate it 180 degrees and it would look the same. When mathematicians list all the ways a particular object is symmetric, they call that list its "group of symmetries," or "group" for short.
2. (Finite) Some groups contain infinitely many symmetries, but some have a specific, finite number of symmetries—possibly very large, but not endless—and so are called "finite groups." For example, the letter T has just two symmetries: a vertical flip, and just doing nothing. (Mathematicians consider doing nothing to

be a symmetry, just as we consider zero to be a number.) On the other hand, a circle like O could be rotated 1 degree, or 2 degrees, or 2.1 degrees, or 2.13 degrees, etc. and still look the same, so it has infinitely many symmetries. The symmetry group of O is therefore infinite, while the symmetry group of T is finite.

3. (Simple) Some groups can be built by multiplying other groups together in a certain way, just as you can build 15 by multiplying 3 by 5. Other groups cannot be built by putting together smaller pieces, just as "prime numbers" like 5 cannot be written as the product of smaller whole numbers. These groups are called "simple groups."

4. (Sporadic) One of the biggest mathematical projects of the 20th century was discovering all the finite simple groups. The project took an international team of mathematicians decades to complete, and the final proof is over 10,000 pages long. Most of the finite simple groups come from infinite "families" of groups which are all simple, in a predictable way, but there are exactly 26 finite simple groups that are called "sporadic" because they belong to no such group. They are simple for their own reasons, on their own terms, without leading to infinitely many relatives.

5. (The Monster) Of those 26 sporadic finite simple groups, the Monster is the largest one. It consists of the 80801742247945128758864599049617107570057 54368000000000 symmetries of a particular 196883-dimensional object; that's more symmetries than there are atoms in the earth.

—Anders Hendrickson, PhD, Department of Mathematics and
Computer Science, Concordia College, Moorhead, Minnesota

More symmetries than there are atoms in the earth.

I turn the airplane back toward Fargo, thinking about the earthquakes in Japan and New Zealand, about the blizzard only days ago and the soft warmth of this afternoon's sky. Measured in kilowatts per square meter, the length of the day and the angle of the sun are heating the snow and soil. The snow is melting. It couldn't be a prettier day to fly. It's also a prelude to disaster. That disaster will give way to summertime, soft light and sunflowers, and tornadoes leaping out of thunderheads. How many ways, I wonder, can I turn this day and see the same thing from the other side?

Is it possible to see the monster's face?

In Winter, the valley farm fields resemble a flat canvas of white crisscrossed with uniform dark lines created by the straight county roads. Bright white after a fresh snow. Warmer weather brings a smooth glaze surface to the snow giving the appearance of water on the horizon. The contrast of the landscape grid pattern is softened by the dark black fields blending in with the county roads. The pattern is there, but not as noticeable.

—E-mail from Mike Paulson, Fargo Flight School manager

Dear Scott,

Last time I gave you a bare-bones mathematical description of what the Monster is. Today's email will be just a few of my thoughts about the Monster and the 25 other sporadic finite simple groups.

As a mathematician, when you start asking how many of a certain thing exist, there are some typical answers. Some objects you search for are unique and isolated, the only ones of their kind. Then again, sometimes the laws of mathematics dictate that there are just a handful of objects of the kind you seek: of Platonic solids, shapes with all identical faces, each face being the same regular polygon, there are exactly five, no more and no fewer.

On the other hand, sometimes the objects you seek are infinitely many, churned out by an endless process. There are infinitely many regular polygons, infinitely many prime numbers, infinitely many complete graphs, and it is no surprise that these should be a dime a dozen, because they're a renewable resource.

What is so surprising to me about the classification of the finite simple groups is their combination of these two. I was not surprised to learn as a student that the infinitely many cyclic groups of prime order are simple, or that all the alternating groups beyond A_4 are simple. These are straightforward processes, each of which can make infinitely many finite simple groups.

But into this mix, this orderly procedure and infinite understanding, come twenty-six oddballs, twenty-six sporadic groups that rear up, finite and simple on their own terms, not as the result of the processes we already understood. The world was almost smooth and predictable—but not quite. The Monster was undoubtedly named for its size, but it and the other 25 are also monstrous in the old sense of the word: prodigies and portents, creatures born unlike their kin, things to be marveled at.

I can never ponder the sporadic groups without thinking of Chesterton's words in Orthodoxy, *that reality is "nearly reasonable, but not quite." The human body is almost symmetric, but not quite; the earth is almost spherical, but not quite. It is said that the exception proves the rule, but the rule is that rules almost always have exceptions. Reality is a portrait, not a diagram.*

Now Chesterton contrasts reality's tendency to admit exceptions with the mathematicians' quest for logic and order, but Chesterton was no mathematician. Even in the heart of pure mathematics, in a realm of thought where observation is nothing and a priori *is everything, even there the very laws of logic insist that in addition to the regular families of finite simple groups there must also be twenty-six exceptions.*

—Anders Hendrickson, PhD, Department of Mathematics and Computer Science, Concordia College, Moorhead, Minnesota

---

When I get back to town, I tell the control tower I'd like to do a few touch-and-go landings, just to stay in good form. The first one is textbook normal.

On the second one, because of incoming traffic, the tower tells me to do a short approach to come in first, which means I get to cut power, dive and bank, and use a word like *swoop* to describe what I'm doing. It's a cowboy landing, movie-style flying, the kind of stuff that makes a pilot smile. For the third landing, because of incoming traffic, I'm told to extend my downwind leg, flying farther away from the runway than usual to let someone else land in front of me. To every horizon, all I see is snow-covered prairie and river and treeline and town. A bit more brown in places. A bit more blue or gray in others. The quality of light has moved. In a day, or a week, or perhaps just a moment, this whole shape will be turned. It will be completely different, and it will be exactly the same.

I land, and as I pull off the runway, I suddenly have a memory of watching *Sesame Street* with my younger brothers. In one cartoon scene, a small child walks into a room. Something large is sleeping in a bed, covered by blankets. The child sees a sign and tries to sound out the words. "Doo-n't bow-ther the mon-ster," he says. He pauses, then reads again, starting to put the syllables together. "Don't bow-ther the monster." He looks at the sign. "Bow-ther?" he asks himself. Slowly, a hand comes out from under the blanket. A huge hand. A gargantuan hand. It wraps around the child so that only his head is visible above the knuckles and fingers. "Bother," a deep voice says. "Don't BOTHER the monster."

I could have it all wrong. It could be *giant* instead of *monster*. But it doesn't matter. It's a scene that's stayed with me for more than forty years.

The child's eyebrows go up. The scene fades to black.

Thin Places and Thick Time

A Duet for Two Worlds

"Ready to go flying?" I ask.

"Absolutely."

"Think I know how to do this?"

Roy Hammerling, a religion professor at the college, sits in the right seat as the Skyhawk enters the runway.

"I'm counting on it," he says.

The throttle goes forward, and the airplane begins to run down the centerline. It's a beautiful day for flying. Clear sky and bright sun. A gentle breeze from the north. Huge distances between the very small clouds. The type of day where chasing an idea with an airplane seems perfectly logical and sane. At 60 knots I ease back on the yoke, the nose lifts, and then the rest of the airplane follows. We begin a gentle climbing turn to the west.

"I love that initial feeling," Roy says. "It's like you're tethered to the ground, and then all of a sudden you break free."

Roy and I are on an expedition this morning, a mission, a voyage of discovery. We are looking for the place where everything changes, the place where the very behavior of the physical earth changes direction. There are signs on the ground that point to the spot, but when you are standing there, the shift is too subtle to see. We are looking for a line reaching back to Pleistocene catastrophe and forward into ecology and myth. We are looking for the Laurentian Divide. And we are looking for something else as well.

Below us the land is green where crops have sprouted, brown where the plants are still emerging. We've had three days of hard rain, and overland water moves toward the Maple and Sheyenne and Red Rivers, streams today in depressions you can measure but never see.

"I am always amazed by the takeoff," he says. "When I was a little kid, I used to imagine it was like there were ropes around the airplane, and you had to break away. And there is this sense of—I don't know—*elation* when you break free."

There is such a thing as accidental genius, I think. Hunting for geology, the normal thing would be to invite a geologist. But the Laurentian Divide in North Dakota is nothing like the Great Divide running the length of the Rocky Mountains. There is no leap and swooning of summit and valley here. Subtle at best, invisible at worst, the Laurentian Divide is more idea than rock, but the evidence of its presence is overwhelming. I mentioned this in a hallway once, and Roy got interested.

If you are looking for the invisible, I think, invite a theologian. I level the wings just fifteen hundred feet over the ground. Traffic on the interstate is light. An egret flies southbound below us.

"I always felt there was a bit of a metaphor for spiritual life in that," Roy continues. "In the sense that what people always want is a sense of joy or happiness. But there's always these things tethering you down to the ground. You can't get away from it. I have a friend who's a pilot, and I've gone up with him a few times. I always have this sense of freedom in flying."

We've begun this conversation a thousand times. In my office, in his office, in hallways and lunch lines, we get to talking about flying and about the small insistent sense that something else is happening beyond the shape of air moving over wings. But then we've always paused.

"*In the airplane,*" I've said. "I want to hear what you think while we're actually flying."

When I told him I was going to try to find the divide, something huge and historic and mostly invisible unless you're looking for it, and even then damn near impossible to fix precisely, it seemed like the perfect opportunity. We've delayed this conversation so long, it nearly erupts.

"Do you know what that means?" he asks. "That feeling at takeoff?"

"Transformation," I say. "It's a leap of faith, perhaps a leap into faith. It's your mind telling your body to relax—the physics and the math work pretty well."

"Some people never get over that fear, though," he says. "Some people can never make that leap. Just like some people sometimes in the religious life never get over certain fears; they build up regulations and walls and rules. They do things that keep them from flying. And it seems to me that the spiritual life is about letting go, is about being free and trusting. There is a sense of mystery about it. There is always a sense of mystery. Like right now, I look over, and you don't even have your hands on the controls."

I smile and point at the autopilot in the panel.

"Oh," he says, laughing. "See? Mystery explained by a higher power."

I remember a map I have at home that shows the rock underneath the Dakota soils. Like nearly every map, it's an aerial perspective. Archean basement rock, billions of years old, from the time when continents first formed and life, nonnucleated single-celled hopes called prokaryotes, first appeared, hides under Fargo. Heading west, however, the rock quickly becomes Cretaceous. The rock of *Tyrannosaurus rex*. The rock of *Giganotosaurus* and *Triceratops*. The rock of Pangaea's breakup. The rock of the Western Interior Seaway, an ocean in the middle of the continent. The rock of a meteor falling on the Yucatán and killing nearly everything. Keep going west and the rock keeps getting younger. But none of it is visible now. The planet cooled. The glaciers came, scraped every hilltop, and filled every valley with gravel and sand. An ice sheet named Laurentide pushed the Missouri River valley into shape. And when the glaciers moved back, the meltwater Lake Agassiz, the largest inland sea in North American history, deposited sediment and clay. There are marks in the North Dakota soil that reveal where icebergs trapped in retreating pack ice scraped the lake-bottom sediment. You cannot see them from the ground.

"You know," I say, "I have been told that there is not one single description in the Bible of an angel in the act of landing. There is one scene where a couple of them are zipping around a living room, but otherwise they are almost always in the air. And if they are on the ground, they are frequently in disguise, appearing as commonplace humans. So it would be possible to argue that their true appearance, the place where they can reveal their true nature, is airborne. It may be forcing the idea a bit, coming from a pilot, but it does strike me that there is something intuitive there. Something true about the human character."

"You can think of Ezekiel being taken up in the fiery chariot, of Jesus's ascending into clouds, and it lends itself to the idea that heaven and the holy are somewhere above."

"These guys don't just dissolve," I say. "They don't just fade away into some other state of being. They rise. They take off. They fly."

"Saint Augustine," Roy says, "in his *Confessions* has this great line. He says something like 'Oh, God, are you the God of the heavens? And if so, are the birds more holy because they fly closer to you?' He knows that God is in some type of heavenly place. But the question is, where is that place?"

"Today," I say, "it's fifteen hundred feet over Dakota farmland."

"Perhaps not," Roy says. "Augustine concludes that the way people need to fly like birds is to go within." He looks out the window. "But I will admit, if Augustine had a Cessna, he might have changed his mind."

I hand Roy the maps we need for today: a pilot's sectional map and a map sent to me by a man named Fred Anderson, a geologist with the North Dakota Geological Survey, showing the line of the divide. I point out the moving map in the airplane's panel and the knob you can turn to zoom in or out. Roy points his camera and then my own out the window. From altitude, the summertime prairie is unexpectedly rich in shades of green and unexpectedly beautiful, too.

"Do you know the Celtic notion of thin places?" Roy asks.

"Not at all," I say.

"Their whole notion is that there are places in this world where this world and the next world, the spiritual world, are in very close proximity. For them it's ponds, groves of oak trees, caves, rivers, oceans. For some reason, it has a lot to do with water. This goes back to their ancient myths about how there was this battle, and the gods and the people were kind of separated in this battle, but the gods left these thin places so that people could move back and forth. These are places where you can get that sense of mystery. Like standing on a cliff leading out into a canyon. You can feel a kind of transcendence there. And I'm serious now—with an airplane you can get that sense of thin place. The whole notion of a thin place is a place where you come close to mystery. You think about who you are, about who the Divine may be, the whole notion of what's eternal, what's temporal, and where those things come together. When you go up in the air, your whole perspective changes."

"I've used the word *grace* before," I say, "to get at this."

"Grace?"

"When you can see that the town over there is connected to the town over there. When you can see that a river joins them, or a line of bluffs protects them both. When you have the aerial perspective to see connections completely invisible on the ground—there is a new understanding, a new insight, a whole new set of patterns and arrangements, a whole new way to see how things depend on each other, a whole new way to think about cause and effect. A whole new perspective on the way mystery is manifest. I know the traditional way to think about grace is that it's undeserved. I know you can't earn it. But what if we think about grace as being one step more fully inside the mystery?"

"That's interesting," Roy says. "But are place and perspective the same thing?"

"Hang on," I say, changing topics. "I need to gain a bit of altitude here."

"Why is that?"

"The airplane measures altitude from sea level, and the ground is getting higher. If I don't climb a bit, we'll fly at precisely the same altitude all the way into the side of one of the Rocky Mountains."

"That wouldn't be good."

Fargo Departure calls, tells me I'm leaving the TRSA (terminal radar service area) and to squawk VFR. I change radio frequency and push in the throttle to climb five hundred feet. The radio is suddenly filled with the voices of pilots self-announcing their positions and their desires at landing fields, it seems like, everywhere.

Roy takes pictures of rivers, farmsteads, shelterbelts, grain bins.

"You get a false sense of security on the ground, don't you?" Roy asks. "You never quite see things clearly. This last spring, for example. You know there's a flood. You know there's water out there. But you can't see it from your home or your office so you don't think about it very much. The pictures on television are an abstraction. But then you fly over it in a plane, and you can see the whole size of the thing, you look out there and you go 'oh, my God . . .'"

A village named Tower City comes up on the left side of the airplane, and I point out the truck stop and the neighborhoods.

"That's amazing," Roy says. "I drive this route all the time."

I point out the wind farm a good way still in front of us, hazy in the distance north of Valley City, and Lake Ashtabula just beyond it.

On the radio, I announce our position twelve miles east of Valley City airport.

We ride quietly for a few moments.

"I like the idea of a thin place," I say. "I mean, look at those towers, those hundreds of towers. You would never see them this way from the ground."

"And even if you were close to it, you wouldn't really see it," Roy says.

"You wouldn't understand its larger scope," I say. "And you would certainly never put those towers into the same sight picture, or *idea,* with these trees off to our left. Our imagination would keep them completely separate. The sky is a complete reshaping of anything we believe about context and connectedness."

The ground has a lot of water standing in fields, slowly working toward the Sheyenne and the James.

"Everything here flows into the Sheyenne," I say, "which flows into the Red, which flows into Hudson Bay. Just in front of us, however, is the spot where everything beyond it flows into the James River, which flows into the Missouri, which flows into the Gulf of Mexico."

"You would expect a sight, wouldn't you?" Roy says.

"This is not where the Laurentide ice sheet ended," I continue. "That's still a good bit farther on. The far side of the Missouri River valley is the pushed-up dirt at the end of the glacier. Did you know that Long Island is really just a big terminal moraine from the same ice sheet? And here, this isn't the old beach line for Lake Agassiz. We passed that a while back. But something in the mechanics of the ice age, something in the way the Laurentide ice sheet moved and withdrew, made this spot the beginning of a slope. A subtle, gentle, invisible slope that changes everything. You could argue that the whole history of human development is based on which way the water flows. It's a bit like gravity," I say. "Gravity is the weakest of the electromagnetic forces, yet it influences every bit of how the universe behaves."

I bank and turn the airplane to the left, to the south, so Valley City will arrive on Roy's side of the airplane. There is a bridge in town, a long trestle for the rail line that spans the valley, and I am hoping for a good picture or two. The Sheyenne River meanders through town, the valley far too wide, it seems, for the apparent flow.

I announce our position south of town, and am about to tell Roy a story about the end of Lake Agassiz, when suddenly there is a voice on the radio I recognize.

"Devil's Lake traffic," he says. "NOAA turbo commander and Twin Otter, two separate aircraft, are over Devil's Lake, surveying at three thousand feet, westbound, about seven miles west of the airport, be advised, Devil's Lake."

Johann!

"The first time I read about thin places, in Celtic myth," Roy says, "I thought, wow—how does this not come through in other myths? And I think it's probably because organized religion has a tendency to want to place God in a place that's easily found. The idea of a thin place hasn't been popular. I mean, the Celts have kept it, and they keep it in a certain type of Catholic Christianity. But for some reason, I think organized religion likes to say, 'Well, this is where you find God, and here's what you do—you go to worship in a church, or you do this or that, and you pray.' But the notion of mystery gets left out of organized religion. Mystery always kind of challenges . . ." He pauses, looks out my window, then points at a solitary wind tower. "Oh! That's the one on the interstate . . ." I can see the look on his face as he connects his own history on the road with his today in the air.

I ask him to take pictures of the Valley City bridge.

"Where is that?"

I point it out to him.

"Oh, I've been under that bridge. And I've been to the monastery that's right over there, too."

Johann announces a climb to ten thousand feet, and I cannot resist the urge to call him.

"Cessna Eight Nine Seven—hey, NOAA, are you going back to Fargo this afternoon?"

There is a pause on the airwaves. Come on, Johann, I say to myself. Answer me.

"These are the Weather Service guys," I tell Roy. "I rode with them last winter."

"Aircraft calling NOAA, say again," Johann says.

"NOAA, this is Cessna Eight Nine Seven, are you returning to Fargo this afternoon?"

"Quite possibly, about five or six p.m.," he says.

"Well," I say, "if this is who I think it is, I hope to be there to say hello."

"How you doing, Scott!" Johann says.

"Pretty good! How are you doing today?"

Roy takes pictures of the bridge.

"Scott, where you flying to today?" Johann asks.

"I am going to try to see the Continental Divide from the air," I say. "So turning south here just west of Valley City."

"Nice."

I decide not to try to explain the notion of a thin place.

"Where are you flying?" I ask.

"Surveying over Devil's Lake," he says.

I will find out later, after we've landed and a day has passed, that what they are doing is called a cosmic-calibration flight. The Twin Otter has just been fitted with the sensing equipment. Flying over the lake removes the background radiation. To measure the invisible and then predict the future, you need to have your instruments tuned.

"I've heard there's some water up there," I say.

"Quite a bit," he says. "Well, catch you later. Fly safe."

"Same for you. Have a good flight."

Valley City diminishes behind us. Just ahead, I can see a spot where the interstate bisects a small lake. Just beyond that, even though I cannot see it from the air, there is a green highway road sign. Continental Divide, it reads. Elevation 1,490. Drivers slow down when they pass that sign, their faces scrunched up in bewilderment.

"This is where you need to start with the maps," I say.

Roy holds the sectional and the map from the ND USGS that shows where the divide should be. I dial the airplane's moving map down to a very small range. We both carry the map of experience in our heads.

"See that lake on my screen?" I ask, pointing at the monitor. "That's this one on your map." I point at the paper.

"Okay, got it."

I point the nose of the airplane downward, and we pick up some speed. We're going to cross a continental divide! Might as well make it dramatic.

"One last thing," Johann calls. "I'm sitting next to a hero . . ."

Paul! I key the microphone and laugh. "Okay, I'm jealous."

The Sheyenne River behind us, I can see the riparian trees that outline the James River in front of us. Somewhere here, I think. Somewhere here.

Say the words *continental divide,* and if there is a map handy, people will point at the Rocky Mountains. Water on one side flows to the Pacific. Water on the other side flows to the Atlantic. It's a clear and simple division, an easy split in the way the geography works. It's also completely wrong. Running the length of the Rockies, from the coastal plains of the Seward Peninsula to Tierra del Fuego, the Great Divide makes the choice between Pacific and other. But not all water on the western side goes to the ocean. The Great Basin is also a divide and collects water from Wyoming to California and sends it no place at all. The Eastern Divide runs the summits of the Appalachians, separating rain for the Atlantic from rain for the Gulf. From Duluth to Chicago, and then up toward Maine, the St. Lawrence Seaway Divide captures the water bound for the St. Lawrence River. In Canada, the Arctic Divide runs northeast from a peak called Snow Dome near Banff and sends the water to the Mackenzie River.

From Triple Peak, a mountain in the Lewis Range in Montana, inside Glacier National Park, the Laurentian Divide begins. Triple Peak is the only place on the planet where a cup of water poured onto the rock would divide itself into three oceans—Pacific, Atlantic, and Arctic. The Laurentian crosses Alberta, Saskatchewan, Montana, North Dakota, South Dakota, Minnesota, Ontario, and Quebec. The Laurentian is the border between Quebec and Newfoundland and Labrador. The Laurentian is the line between the Labrador Sea and Hudson Bay. In Minnesota, the Ojibwe called the Laurentian *Mesabi.* Sleeping Giant. The Laurentian was the northern border of the Louisiana Purchase.

"You can't see anything here, can you?" I ask. "There's no rise, no ridge. Nothing."

"Nothing," Roy says, looking out his window.

"But something happens here," I say. "Something in the landscape changes. Something that was created when the ice sheet withdrew."

Roy holds up the USGS paper, then turns it upside down so it matches our course.

"Are you trying to just go straight at it?" he asks.

"I'm trying to find any bit of it, any sight of it at all."

"It's amazing that it's such a monumental shift, and due to something that was here so long ago."

I see a line between two wetlands on my side and put the airplane into a steep turn to the left so I can bring it up on Roy's side. When we arrive, I put the airplane into a steep turn to the right, and Roy takes pictures straight down. I half expect him to say something about the turns, but his gaze is glued outside.

"Do you know how Lake Agassiz ended?" I ask. "Do you know that story?"

"I'm not sure I do."

"The Laurentide ice sheet is retreating," I say, "and on the south side there is this huge lake of meltwater. Lake Agassiz. It is the largest inland sea in North America. Three hundred and sixty-five thousand square miles, give or take a few. And the whole thing began in the Red River valley. That's where the first parts of the lake were formed. Part of the meltwater drained south, past the Traverse Gap and into the Minnesota River. As the lake grew, it drained through the Great Lakes, and eventually it drained down the Mackenzie. It drug the icebergs that left those scars in the soil.

"This is woolly mammoth time," I say. "There are people around, but this is pre-Dorset Canada. This is nine thousand years ago."

Roy looks at the maps in his hands.

"Now imagine the whole thing falling apart. Not over time, but all at once. There was an ice dam in Canada, up near Hudson Bay, holding back the lake water, and it collapsed. The equivalent of fifteen Lake Superiors draining through that gap in a couple months. Because it was all freshwater suddenly entering the northern oceans, it's been identified as the cause of a huge global climate shift. Sea levels all over the planet would have risen so much, some people think this one event may be the reason nearly every culture on earth has a flood story in their mythic past. It is possible to argue that this collapse caused the break between the Mediterranean and the Black Seas. Sea levels rose so much, the event caused a massive resettlement of human culture."

"Amazing."

"The ice dam would have been in Canada, but we're at the back end of the lake here. We're flying over the site of one of the largest geological, climate-shift disasters the planet has ever known. And somewhere right below us, right now, is the spot where the flood-from-God story starts. A drop of water goes one way or the other. Either Hudson Bay or the Gulf of Mexico."

"Wow."

"See those grain bins in front of us?"

"Yes."

"See that one tree standing alone out in front of them?"

"Yes."

"According to our map, that one tree may be as close as we're going to get to figuring out where it is."

We fly over the tree, an oak tree, and then we turn south. On our maps, there is a line leading from here that shows where the divide should be. But there is no ridge, no Mesabi Range rich in iron ore. There isn't so much as a hill.

"Can you see anything?" I ask. "Anything in the land at all that shows a change?"

We fly over the Stoney Slough National Wildlife Refuge. We fly over Bear Creek. I point at a lake and an outlet stream that flow into the Sheyenne. We turn hard left and right again, looking down for any sign or clue.

"If we are just a little bit west of Bear Creek," I say, "we should be right over the Continental Divide. Right here. Right now. Thirty-five hundred feet, 96 knots. A clear summer day in June. And the whole thing is invisible. Absolutely invisible. All you can see are its effects."

Roy looks at the USGS map and directs me down the western edge of the creek. We pick up a small tailwind, and our speed increases.

We come up on the town of Kathryn much faster than I expect and certainly faster than I hope. We find the town of Hastings on the map and fly to touch the west side of town. We see creek beds heading east.

"Help me look," I say. "Do we see anything at all?"

"It's just wetlands," Roy says.

"No, if you look, you can see which way the water flows, you can see the shape of the drainage."

"That's true!"

"On your side of the airplane, it drains to the south. On my side of the airplane, it drains to the north. There's no ridge, but look at the shape of the places where water is moving. It's all evidence. You can't see it directly, but you can see what it causes."

We both laugh.

"I love Emerson's quote from *Nature*," I say. "'Why not have a religion of revelation to us?'"

"Emerson being a transcendentalist and interested in the mystical—that gets us back to the whole notion of thin places and trusting mystery as opposed to knowing it clearly," Roy says. "Even though we're relying on a lot of science to keep us up in the air, the science of flying and the emotion of flying are two different things."

We fly the line south, but time begins to press on us both. We turn east, toward home, a broad, sweeping gentle bank of the airplane.

"I love turns," I say.

It would be easy to feel defeated, I think. In truth, however, I feel exactly the opposite.

"The other thing we haven't talked about goes with thin places," Roy says. "It's the notion of thick time. I don't know about you, but even though I know we've been up here for only about an hour, it feels like a lot longer. There is that sense of time slowing down. Everything in our normal lives militates against slowing down. It's always speeding things up. Tasks, things that take you outside of yourself, things that don't give you much joy, committee meetings, all those sorts of things. But when you get into a space where the distractions of the world can't demand anything of you, like something as simple as not having your cell phone, then you live more in the moment. And as you're more attentive to the moment, all of a sudden time becomes very thick, and it slows very, very down. It's like the old story about when you have an accident or a moment of crisis—you can almost watch that moment happen in slow motion. All the details are right there. It's because you're so attentive to the moment. The Buddhists call it mindfulness. It might be a certain type of meditation in a variety of Christian traditions. But this whole notion of thick time fits very well with what we're doing in the sky today. And both thin places and thick time are really tied to the heart of what religion is all about, or what faith or what mystery is about. It's when you think about what's significant in life, what's meaningful, what's important. When thin places and thick time accompany one another, those are the moments you really don't want to lose."

"When those two things do come together, is there a word for that? Is that grace? Is that insight? Is that what?"

"I would call it mystery."

We cross the Sheyenne River and fly over farmsteads, shelterbelts, grain bins, and county roads.

"The monks would say to do everything mindfully," Roy says. "They say wash your dishes mindfully. I don't want to do that. I want to get that task over as quickly as possible. But then they would say I'm throwing a part of my life away."

"I have a friend," I say, "a theologian out in California who studies the Desert Fathers, the early-second-century monastics. He says their idea was first to remove themselves from what they called their passions. Remove themselves from the daily, mundane, trivial demands on our souls. Only after that, they said, could they begin an appreciation of the physical world. And only after that, they said, could they begin to approach an understanding of God."

"Remember what Saint Benedict says," Roy answers. "'We retreat from the world in order to change it.'"

"One of my favorite quotes is by Saint-Exupéry," I say. "He says, 'Contrary to the vulgar illusion, it is thanks to the metal, and by virtue of it, that the pilot rediscovers nature. As I have already said, the machine does not isolate man from the great problems of nature but plunges him more deeply into them.'"

"The Celtic monks, the Buddhists, they are all looking for a way to make every place thin and every time thick. That's what Whitman does. That's what Emerson does. And you pilots, you get it all the time. There's a great moment in the play *Camelot,* after Merlin turns Arthur into a bird, when he returns and says he realized there were no boundaries, no dukedoms, only people longing for justice, longing for a good life. In the end, that's all it's all about."

The airplane carries us back to Fargo and a fine smooth landing.

"We did not find the Laurentian Divide," I say as we turn onto short final approach.

"No," Roy says, "but we knew we wouldn't when we began."

Deep SWE

Day One

Of course, it has to be a fluid that keeps us on the ground.

Standing in a hangar at the Fargo Jet Center, two NOAA pilots, Johann Gebauer and Paul Hemmick, WDAY television meteorologist Daryl Ritchison and his photographer, and I are all staring at an airplane wing. We are supposed to be in the sky already. It's midmorning in early February, eastern North Dakota. We are supposed to be in the sky, measuring the amount of water in the snowpack, the snow-water equivalent, the SWE. The numbers are supposed to be sent to the National Weather Service's River Forecast Centers. The numbers will tell us about the floods we all know are coming to the Sheyenne River and the Red River of the North. The floods that are coming to Fargo, Moorhead, Grand Forks, Winnipeg. This is important work. The weather is perfect. Cold and clear and calm. No ceiling. Unlimited visibility. A day made for flying. But the airplane is broken. The scavenge pump is dead.

"Scavenge pump?" I ask.

"It moves fuel from the outboard fuel cell to the inboard fuel cell when the level is low," Johann says. "The airplane has a five-hour range, and we're scheduled for a three-hour flight. We're not going to need it. But we can't fly with a broken pump unless the office signs off on it."

The fluid, the jet fuel, won't move on its own. We can't make it move because the pump is broken. Outside, the water won't move either. It's frozen in place and frozen to the ground. Daryl and I stare at the airplane, a Gulfstream Jet Prop Commander. Twin engine, high wing, it's a fine airplane for looking at the ground. It all makes perfect sense.

Johann makes a call on his cell phone to the NOAA Aircraft Operations Center at MacDill Air Force Base in Tampa, Florida. Both men, young and dark-haired, dressed in blue flight suits, seem annoyed at the delay. NOAA is part of the Department of Commerce, yet they use navy rank. Outside the airplane, Johann is an ensign, and Paul is a lieutenant. But inside the airplane, Johann has more flight time, and he is the aircraft commander. Paul is the co-pilot. They trade who sits in the left seat.

Paul walks by and raises an eyebrow. "We might fly today. We might not," he says.

Time is slipping by. We are supposed to fly up to the Devil's Lake basin today. That snow is deep, dangerous in what it means downstream. There is another mission on the docket for a flight south, a look at the Minnesota side of the Red River, so if the airplane is fixed fast, we might go that way.

Daryl and I follow the two men into the Jet Center terminal. Daryl sends his photographer away. There's nothing to do but wait, stare at the snow and sky, and wish we were flying. So we find coffee, a table, and some chairs. Outside the sun is bright on the snowfields.

"It's the switch," Johann says. "Activation of this switch is manual when there is around three hundred pounds of Jet A remaining inside each of the tanks. The purpose of the scavenge pump is to get any fuel remaining in the outboard fuel cells to flow into the inboard cells. But the light is on all the time now. That doesn't mean the pumps are running. There is a short keeping the light on even though the switch and pumps are selected off. So, basically, we need it fixed because if we went flying and the right pump doesn't turn on, we wouldn't know since the light is on regardless."

There are people at the River Forecast Centers waiting on these numbers. There are people in the Weather Service waiting for what the numbers mean. There are city officials planning how many sandbags to fill. There are school-children filling sandbags. It's only February. Insurance companies are pushing flood insurance.

"It's possible they can fix it," Paul says. "If not, we can overnight the part, and we can trade it out and fly tomorrow."

I look over at Daryl. We've known each other for years. Tall and thin with sand-colored hair, he's the kind of meteorologist who chases tornadoes. Solid science and a bit of adrenaline. He can't wait to get in the airplane.

"Tell me how the scanner works?" I ask.

"What's in there now," Johann says, "is a gamma-radiation detector. It's a passive detector. It's got its own computer and a series of crystals—downward-facing crystals and upward-facing crystals—and we measure the upwelling gamma radiation. The naturally occurring gamma radiation, coming out of the top twenty centimeters of soil. The radiation that's been coming out of the ground for forever, for billions of years."

"Got it," I tease. "We're going to blast the countryside with radiation from a low-flying airplane."

"No," Johann smiles. "It's a passive system. We're not actively sending out any radiation. We're simply absorbing it; it's a gathering of isotope signatures. We're looking at potassium, uranium, and thorium. Those are the three main isotopes that we're really concentrating on. These are the core isotopes that were discovered to allow us to measure the snow-water equivalent. The SWE."

"How does it all get processed?" Daryl asks.

Paul leans forward. "As for collecting it," he says, "there's a data-processing unit that's going to actually be computing the SWE value. It's also going to take into consideration certain coefficients, not only with the crystals but within the radiation detector, and also interference with the aircraft. Then we're also setting the outside temperature because there is a mass of air that the isotopes have to travel through. So we're inputting things into the data-processing unit, the data-processing unit is making those calculations airborne, and then at the end of the day, we're going to process those because as we fly those flight lines, we're also writing comments, such as, 'Deep drifts,' or 'Source river open at this point, not frozen.' Once we FTP this stuff that night to the NOHRSC office, that's the National Operational Hydrologic Remote Sensing Center, in Minneapolis, that's then distributed to whoever uses it. The River Forecast Centers and the hydrologists at the forecast centers, they're able to plug our information into their flood-outlook models. You have ground observers and you have the satellites, and we basically fill in the gaps. The satellite is a broad picture, doesn't give you much detail, and when you look at the people taking their own little SWE samples in their backyard, that's a very localized thing. A lot of places are very sparsely populated, so what we're doing is we're going out and getting that fifteen- to twenty-nautical-mile stretch, a thousand feet wide."

We watch a jet take off, a couple private planes come and go. We watch students and their instructors in white Cessna 172s get a feel for the flare. We are sitting in a conference room, waiting to go. It strikes me that NOHRSC is pronounced like "no risk," which makes me smile.

Johann's cell phone rings. Daryl and I sit up, suddenly hopeful.

"We might still fly today," Paul says. "But it's looking doubtful. We're losing daylight."

Daryl calls his photographer and offers an update.

The airplane is warm inside the hangar. The coffee is strong. Somewhere in Tampa, someone is deciding the risk of letting this airplane fly. We're told that it might be possible to simply disconnect the pump and placard the switch as inoperative, sign a waiver, and get on with it. We wait, and we get to talking about history. Paul says he went to sea when he joined NOAA, was the navigation officer on the *Oregon II,* then worked as an admiral's aide in Washington, DC. Then he had to make a decision. Either back to sea or take up something completely new. He took to the air. Off the phone, no news yet, Johann says he studied aviation and meteorology in college, became a flight instructor and pumped gas at a FBO (fixed-base operation), flew for Delta's Comair, and then jumped over to NOAA. Together, they fly the prairie, and they also fly the Brooks Range in northern Alaska. They do harbor-seal surveys in southeastern Alaska during summer. "Because of television," Johann says, "my mother thinks I'm flying blind in Alaska storms, almost hitting hills."

"But you fly very low," I say. "Five hundred feet above the ground is nothing."

"Once you are exposed to that environment," Johann continues, "you begin to feel comfortable with that environment, and there are measures that we take to ensure safety. Like I mentioned before, we have a waiver that allows us to fly at five hundred feet anywhere in the country. Canada, too. We have a military planning software called FalconView. It's a DOD program that basically displays sectional charts, and even more detail as we go through the layers of maps and scales of maps of where we are flying over. You are able to highlight obstructions before you go."

"When we're surveying at five hundred feet, we have to maintain between 100 and 120 knots ground speed," Paul says. "If we're not surveying, it would be about 250 knots true airspeed. Those planes have to survey between 100 and 120 knots ground speed, which is what the systems are calibrated to. It allows us to collect the most data that we can and maintain safety. Any slower, and we are jeopardizing our own safety."

Five hundred feet above the ground at only 115 knots. Pilots call it flying low and slow. All things considered, it's the most dangerous way to fly. Make a mistake, and you're inside somebody's bean field fast.

"Is there a favorite flight?" I ask. "One that is just a better story?"

Paul laughs. "Johann?"

Johann says, "It actually doesn't even involve a Snow Survey. This summer we were doing a national geodetic survey, a gravity survey, all over the state of Alaska. Gravity for the redefinition of the American vertical datum. We were flying all over Alaska, checking gravity, just basically cruising along between twenty and twenty-five thousand feet for four hours straight, two times a day, so eight hours a day, all summer long. I got to see a lot of the terrain in Alaska, which was pretty neat. But as far as surveying, when we survey in the Kenai Peninsula in Alaska, around south of Anchorage toward Homer, Seward area, that's a really pretty area to fly in."

"Just a couple of weeks ago, we were out here surveying North Dakota," Paul says, "and Daryl, you might remember low, low ground fog to the point where you couldn't even see the ground? So we're flying at five hundred feet, and this low, low ground fog is just hovering over the surface. We really can't even see streets, but we're surveying because we have our moving maps. And that was really odd to me, because if you're flying VFR, visual, those are your reference points. We could see the ground, barely, and we were safe; we maintain safety at all times. But, you know, that kind of sticks up in my mind. We're on top, as if the fog was clouds, but we can survey. It was very pretty."

We wait, drink more coffee, watch other airplanes take off and land. When the phone rings, the news is not good. The part will be here in the morning, but we cannot fly today. The disappointment is heavy in the room.

"It is an awesome plane to fly," Johann says. "They are really awesome planes to fly."

Day Two

At system check, the airplane bucks like a racehorse in a starting gate, every muscle wanting to go. Paul flying left seat, Johann flying right seat, I sit in the middle, just behind the scanner, and Daryl sits in back. The temperature is twelve degrees below zero, Fahrenheit. The windchill is minus thirty. The sky is clear. A great day for flying. We all want to get into the air.

We've finished the safety briefing, what to do in event of fire, how to use the oxygen, how to exit the airplane. Paul and Johann go through the checklists like a well-tuned pair. I turn around and look at Daryl. "I am totally stoked for this!" he says, a wide grin on his face.

Earlier, we played a terrible joke. Just by coincidence, Paul and Johann and I arrived at the Jet Center at the same time. The airplane was towed onto the ramp, and the pilots began the preflight checks. Daryl's photographer showed up. Daryl had one last segment to do on air this morning, so we knew he would be the last to arrive. But as we saw his pickup on the Jet Center road, we suddenly had a plan. We hid around a corner in a very dark room. When he came in, with the straightest face possible, a woman named Tabitha, who was working the Jet Center desk, calmly informed Daryl that we had left. She said there was a weather problem, and we couldn't wait. For just an instant, you could feel the despair fill the room. But Daryl is not that easily fooled, and we all came around the corner laughing.

At the same time, a young woman, college age, stood a bit hesitantly near the desk for a while, then asked if this is where the flight lessons started. The excitement and nervousness of it all poured out of her face and smile. Tabitha directed her one building over, to the flight school.

Now, watching the auxiliary power unit being wheeled away from the NOAA plane, we can see her getting her first walk around and preflight of a Cessna 172. And what I wish I could tell her is the joy never goes away. What she's feeling today, she will feel when she solos, when she passes her check ride, and every time she takes an airplane into the sky.

At 9:46 a.m. we are cleared for takeoff on Runway Two-Seven. Engines and props set to full forward, brakes released, and this plane bolts down the runway. Acceleration, I believe, is always a thrill. It doesn't matter if it's quick feet, a fast car, or a hot airplane. Acceleration is an expression of both power and desire. It's impossible not to smile.

Rotation and we are airborne. The gear come up before we clear the end of the runway. We make a right turn, toward the northwest, but then we have to halt our climb. The gear are up, but a panel light says they may not be locked in the up position. When it's this cold, Johann tells us, sometimes ice gets in the sensor. We're going to cycle the gear down and back up. The gear go down and lock, then come up and lock. Everything looks good, and we're on our way.

We pass the Sheyenne River, then the South Branch of the Elm River. We bank left to give the University of North Dakota Aerospace flight-school practice areas a wide berth, self-announcing to practice areas named Kilo and Golf. We're covering a lot of ground very fast. Outside of Mayville, riparian trees outline the hard turns and meanders of the Goose River. Johann takes photos, GPS stamped with time and location so hydrologists can look at the photos and correlate them with the survey scanner readings. From one horizon to every other, the Red River valley is as flat as a speedboat's dream.

"Everyone ready for the first line?" Paul asks.

The town of Northwood is off to our right. We descend to five hundred feet above the ground. The air temperature is set into the machine. The flaps come down to their first setting, twenty degrees, and the nose goes up. Classic slow flight. High power, high drag, high lift, high angle of attack—slow speed in the sky.

One of the truths of flying is that most airplanes *want* to fly. Every bit of their shape and design, every function of their instruments and controls, is a way to make flying the easiest state for the machine to achieve. That's why, after landing, airplanes are often tied to the ground. A breeze comes along, and the thing wants to leap into the sky. Speed and altitude are what keep you alive.

If there is a danger to flying, it has little to do with high and fast. It has everything to do with low and slow. Too slow, and you've prevented a wing from being a wing. Too low, and there isn't any room to recover from your stall. Pilots who receive spin training—how to recover when the airplane points its nose at the earth and revolves around itself—are told right at the beginning that no amount of spin training will help you if you overcorrect in slow flight low. If you overshoot your turn to final approach, and you try to bring the airplane into line by steepening the bank, you'll stall, then spin, then die because the earth rises faster than you can correct the spin.

Slow flight is something you learn in your early lessons. It's not how fast you can go. It's the talent for holding the airplane just above how slow it can go.

The survey machine, the black box itself, is silent. No whirrs, no bells, not even a click or a flashing light. Just crystals doing their crystal thing, measuring the radiation that has been coming out of the soil for as long as the planet has been spinning, measuring the changes brought on by water in the snow. Measuring, I think to myself, how many sandbags we are going to need to fill, how many clay dikes we are going to need to build.

The first survey line is about fifteen miles long, just north of a county road. The airplane rides steady and true through the air. "This is beautiful," we all say at one point or another. We can see the plowed road, the buried fence lines, the trees looking alone.

We pass over lakes and farm ponds, invisible except for the outlined depression of the shore in the snowfields.

It's 10:20 in the morning, and the first survey line ends. Flaps come up, power goes up, we gain a bit of altitude on our way to the next run.

Nine point one centimeters. About three inches of water in the snowpack.

"Is that a lot for this time of year?" I ask.

"Yes," Johann says. "But that's not one of the larger measurements this year."

"Normally we have only about two inches this time of year," Daryl says.

Low end for this winter. High end for history. This is not a good sign for spring.

"We've seen four and a half to five inches of water in places this year," Johann says.

"That's really not good," Daryl says, mostly to himself.

Our next line is from the town of Hamar to Warwick. It takes us no time to get there. Stump Lake passes off the right side, and Johann takes pictures out his window. The Sheyenne River passes off to the left. So many roads are covered, so many sections more hinted at than revealed, the land looks embossed, I think.

"No threats," Johann tells Paul. What he means is no cell phone or electrical towers, no cables or power lines, nothing reaching far enough up into the sky to snag this airplane out of its path. We go back down to five hundred feet. In creek beds and farmyards, I can see marks left by snowmobiles and by children's boots. There are bare spots where the wind has blown the snow away from the ground. In other places there are tremendous drifts on the shadowed side of treelines, buildings, anything at all.

"Twelve centimeters," Johann says. The computer in his lap gives him instant survey numbers. Almost five inches of water! From three to five inches of water in just ten miles of travel. We could have flown over a small depression, a small valley, just a shallow spot—anything that would cause the snow to fill in the void. But it doesn't really matter. Five inches of water is holding there, waiting for the days to warm. We pass red barns in white snow. One type of island now. Another type of island very soon.

We climb again and turn to the northwest. The next run is Devil's Lake to Churchs Ferry, and we have to cross the lake itself to get there. Over Devil's Lake is just like being over the clouds. White and flat to every horizon. You can see the trees at the shoreline, yet they almost seem made up. It's a bit like looking at a photographic negative. The lake area, covered in snow and ice, is impossible to ignore. The simple huge size of the ice. The simple huge weight of the snow. For some reason, a single snow-blowing tractor cuts a path across the lake.

The run begins. Smooth air. Paul flies the airplane while the rest of us try to make sense of the view. The run ends. Eleven point four centimeters. Nearly four and a half inches. We turn right, back east a bit. "Some lonely farmsteads out here," I say. Everyone nods.

"Everyone knows the NOAA Hurricane Hunters," Johann says. "But in terms of financial impact, the Snow Survey is second only to them."

All the snow, I think, from Atlantic to Pacific. All the flights, all the numbers, all the forecasts. If the Hurricane Hunters are the Hollywood car chase, the Snow Survey is the methodical detective searching out clues.

The next line is Garske to Starkweather. On the way there, I point out wind patterns on the ice fields below us, straight lines of snow blown clear to reveal the glossier shine of ice, and ask Daryl if that's just accidental or if they reveal some history. "That is interesting," he says.

"Maybe just some wind gusts," Johann says.

We all stare out the windows at the snow.

"No threats," Johann says.

"Garske in sight," Paul says.

The run begins.

"Actually," Johann says, "that may be because of some melting. You can see the reflection out there."

Johann takes a picture of a UPS truck on a gravel road. "I took a picture of a Budweiser truck yesterday," he says. "I took that specifically for one of our pilots. He was a Budweiser truck driver for a while in St. Louis."

"After this one, Paul," Johann says, "we'll blast down to Lakota, then we'll fly north up to, uh, up toward this way." Johann points to the moving map and sectional charts on the aircraft panel. "Then we'll head back over toward the Red."

"Blast?" I think to myself. When your work is in slow flight, it makes perfect sense.

The last run was 11.3 centimeters. Four point four inches of water.

We pass a holding area for railway cars, lumber carriers, then head toward Edgeland, and then toward Rolla. I find myself wondering about North Dakota town names—Starkweather, Edgeland—and wondering what early history, what bad weather and desperation, led to those names.

"Pretty soon we'll start heading over toward Langdon and Cavalier," Johann says.

Between the two there is what's called a "Perimeter Area Radar." Paul and Johann have a special supplement to their charts that shows the location. On civilian charts, all that's noted is "buildings." On the NOAA chart it says "Perimeter Area Radar. Avoid!" This is the radar that can see over the horizon and waits for the Russian missiles.

"We'll fly to the south of it," Paul says.

"Just saw a pheasant flying out of one of the marshes down there," Daryl says.

Next line is 11.1 centimeters. More than 4 inches of water.

We pass a square of chain-link fence, the unmistakable signature of an old nuclear missile silo. A few seconds later we pass another.

Another run starts.

"This is good deer habitat," Paul says.

We look out the windows, and it seems there are a million deer in Edmore. In the treelines, in backyards, in parking areas, in the fields, and on the roads leaving town. Not one of us can say why. It's just a fact, an observation, one of those things that make you wonder, then ask why. Much like wondering how much water is in the snow.

The math is not comforting.

1 square mile, 1 inch deep in water = 2,323,200 cubic feet.

2,323,200 x 4 inches (the average so far today) = 9,292,800 cubic feet.

9,292,800 cubic feet converts to 69,514,971.43 gallons.

The flow rate of Niagara Falls is 6 million cubic feet per minute.

It would take a minute and a half for Niagara to empty just 1 square mile of prairie.

All by itself, the Sheyenne River drains nearly 10,000 square miles.

It would take Niagara ten days to drain the Sheyenne River Basin.

Seven point two centimeters on the last run. Two point eight inches of water.

It's difficult to look at the snow, to think about the water and the floods, then look at the airplane and not feel a kind of awe. Not because these guys are the Blue Angels or the Thunderbirds. They are not. But this is solid work, essential work, and not just inspiration or entertainment. This is slow flight, day after day, while a silent machine absorbs isotopes and a computer gathers numbers. Those numbers call entire cities to action.

"So, Paul," I call from the back, remembering a story he told about the claim of an overly enthusiastic reporter, "*are* you guys the heroes of government aviation?" His shoulders visibly slump in the pilot's seat. "Oh, no," he says. "I hope that doesn't get quoted."

We get set up for the next run. Johann calls out a five-hundred-foot tower. "Go north, then a little dogleg," he says.

Johann talks about how the airplane really does need pretty good weather to fly. Not because of safety, but because of the survey. "It can be marginal, but it really needs to be pretty good for us to fly. Sometimes we get caught right in the middle of a high-pressure system," he says, "and the winds are all over the place. Headwind, then tailwind, then crosswind. Line to line we can't get the winds we need."

We pass an old-fashioned windmill, a derelict barn. "I wonder what the history is here," I say.

Snow has drifted across the county road. A combine stands frozen and snow covered in a field. Johann points out some massive drifts in the lee of a treeline along a railroad, then takes a picture. "I don't really know what the hydrologists see in those drifts," he says. "But they want pictures of drifts, of fresh snow in trees, if the river is frozen or open, if there is ice in the river, all sorts of things."

I ask if they ever take the hydrologists along for flights.

"Sometimes," Paul says. He once took a "high-level guy" who wanted to look at Devil's Lake. During the spring melt they take observers along. They know exactly where all the gauges are in the rivers.

Twelve point five centimeters. Four point nine inches of water.

"Next line is where?" Paul asks.

"Due east," Johann says.

"Coming right, due east, tower in sight," Paul says.

We begin a line near Robertson, heading toward Langdon.

"Is Langdon where the pyramid is?" Paul asks.

The pyramid is an old radar and missile site from the Cold War.

"Yep," says Daryl.

"We'll have to look for that."

We settle into a routine. We approach a line. Paul calls out the temperature. Johann calls out threats, if there are any. Paul lowers the flaps, adjusts the power and props. Both men check ground speed. Johann holds the laptop computer and starts and stops the scanner. Paul flies the airplane. When the line is done, the flaps go up, the power goes up, and we blast to the next line.

On one line, at five hundred feet, Paul says, "Oh, here you go. Here are some cows. Let's see what they do. They might raise their head. They usually just ignore us."

We all watch out the windows to see if a Gulfstream Jet Prop Commander can scare a cow. Not one of them looks up.

"It looks like, 'I don't care,'" Johann says.

We scan near Langdon. "I think I can see that pyramid off to the right," Daryl says.

"Can you?" Johann asks.

"Follow the road, off to the right," Daryl says.

Paul banks the airplane in that direction.

"Is it right there?" Paul asks.

"Yes," Daryl replies.

"There it is, we got it," Paul says.

A pyramid rises from the North Dakota snow. Flat on top, you would almost think it's some type of funky grain elevator. What we cannot see are the missile hatches. Spartan and Sprint missiles, hoped-for interceptors long before Reagan's missile defense program. Nuclear missiles. What we cannot see is the size of the project underground. This is a place that was supposed to *survive* a nuclear attack. There are a power plant and a reservoir underground. The cavern is so large, it's said to make its own weather.

"It's deactivated?" Johann asks.

"I'm not sure it ever was in service," Daryl says. "I was told it was built just to get the Russians to sign the START treaty."

We pass just to the east of the building, take pictures.

"Pretty scary looking," Paul says.

The air base in Minot is still a nuclear-ready base. The air base in Grand Forks no longer has the bomb, but they have the UAVs, the unmanned aerial vehicles. The launch tubes for the ICBMs of the Cold War have been imploded all over the state; only the small squares of chain-link fence remain. On the Web, the site south of Langdon is being offered for redevelopment.

The last couple lines are easy. Paul points out some huge drifts. We all watch the way the earth changes shapes and shadows in the snow. At one point, Paul asks Johann if we can do a "Snow Survey turn." I smile at this, knowing he means a steep turn, a small thrill in the sky. Johann says no, nothing that steep.

"Massive drifts," Johann calls out. "You could build a snow cave in there so easily."

"Is that a project?" Paul asks.

"Sure."

The last line is Grafton to St. Thomas.

When they are done, we climb and blast our way home. We fly over some thin clouds and follow the Red River, frozen and bright and outlined by trees. Paul gives us a scenic tour of Fargo on our approach, and the landing is smooth and soft.

There are numbers in the machine. As soon as Johann is in the terminal, the numbers light-speed their way to the NOHRSC office, and from there they join the great computer prediction models. But right now they are simply data. Observations of isotopes leaving the ground. They are nothing less, however, than a crystal ball. A peculiar way to see the future.

The report on the 10:00 p.m. news, and again the next morning, begins with Daryl standing at the edge of the Red River, talking about the SWE, the amount of water in the snow. We see a man collect snow in a measuring tube on the ground, then melt the snow to see how much water it holds. Then we cut to the airplane taxi and takeoff. There are shots of the scanner, of Paul and Johann at the flight controls, of Daryl looking out a window, of the snow and ice below the airplane, of the airplane's reflection in the polished spinner in front of a prop as we land. The SWE is called the single most important number in the flood forecast. Daryl explains how the airplane needs to fly only five hundred feet above the ground. He does not say it was a dangerous flight, nor does he say it was beautiful. He does not mention the sheer size of the open space, the thousand colored shades of snow on the prairie. On camera Paul, a hero of government aviation, explains the radiation detector. The TV station gives Daryl two minutes for his report, nearly twice the length of a normal report.

A couple days later, the final report on the NOHRSC website gives the data. Eleven runs over the prairie in eastern North Dakota.

:TO ——— Service Hydrologist (Please give HARDCOPY to SH)
:FROM —— Andy Rost, Minneapolis, Minnesota
:Visit our web page at http://www.nohrsc.noaa.gov
:SUBJECT—AIRBORNE SNOW WATER EQUIVALENT DATA 110207155906
:————————————————————————————
: Total No. of flight lines sent = 11
:————————————————————————————
:Line Survey %SC SWE SWE %SM Est Fall %SM Pilot
:No. Date (in) (35%) (M) Typ Date (F) Remarks

```
:=====================================================
ND204 DY110207 / 100 / 4.5 : 5.4, 53 101105 53 , 0
ND208 DY110207 / 100 / 4.0 : 3.8, 31 101107 31 , 0
ND212 DY110207 / 100 / 2.9 : 3.1, 41 101105 40 , 0 ground ice, deep sn
ND213 DY110207 / 100 / 4.4 : 4.3, 34 101107 34 , 0 ground ice, deep sn
ND217 DY110207 / 100 / 3.5 : 2.6, 20 101107 20 , 0 ground ice, some bare gnd
ND219 DY110207 / 100 / 3.6 : 2.9, 23 101107 23 , 0 ground ice, nice dfts
ND220 DY110207 / 100 / 3.4 : 2.9, 26 101107 25 , 0 ground ice, nice dfts
ND224 DY110207 / 100 / 4.7 : 4.2, 25 101105 24 , 0
ND227 DY110207 / 100 / 3.6 : 3.3, 29 101107 29 , 0 lrg dfts, bare gnd, gnd ic
ND230 DY110207 / 100 / 4.9 : 4.7, 32 101107 31 , 0 some ground ice, deep sn
ND231 DY110207 / 100 / 4.4 : 4.1, 28 101105 28 , 0 ground ice evident
.END
```

High SWE values noted around Devils Lake area. Completed lines west and north-west of GFK [Grand Forks]. Large drifts, ground ice, and deep snow observed.

Bare ground was observed following latest freezing rain event. We are unable to fly ND239 due to air traffic constraints.

One hundred percent snow cover. Three to four and a half inches of water in the snow. Everywhere. All of it soon to melt into the Red River basin. All of it soon to seep, to run, to flow. But nothing about the beauty and grace of a bright winter day. Nothing about herds of deer or the towers of national defense. Nothing about the sight of frozen rivers meandering through flatlands on their way to Hudson Bay. Nothing about a fast airplane flying low and slow. Nothing about the isotopes of potassium, uranium, and thorium. Nothing about the lives of men who fly these paths to collect the numbers. Just the SWE. Just the measurement that will measure how badly hell will break loose come spring.

A couple days later, the front page of the *Forum,* the newspaper in Fargo, reads: "The River Will Rise: Area Flood Forecast Takes Ominous Turn."

Collecting the Horizon

1.

Just a whisper will do.

You hear it down the hall, part of a conversation that does not include you, and you lean to follow the sounds as they round a corner. Or you remember the lyric to a song you knew when you were young and feel your imagination swell with the weight of a dream on the edge of being gone too long. Or you read something, and, much later, you wonder why one detail stays with you. It wasn't important to the story. It's become essential to you now. So you begin to chase it, to follow it, to bring it close, to find out why.

Or you simply keep it, store it in your head and heart. The details matter. It may take years for a pattern to emerge or for the meaning to appear. The pattern may never emerge and the meaning may never appear, yet the details carry weight. This is important. It does not matter why.

2.

"Cessna Two Four One Two Whiskey, Runway Three-Six at Bravo Three intersection, turn left on course, cleared for takeoff."

"Cleared for takeoff, One Two Whiskey," I say.

The throttle goes in. Jonathan, in the seat next to me again, chart on a clipboard on his lap, camera at the ready, smiles at the beginning rush. There is some rain to the west and south, but the sky at Fargo is only dotted with cotton-ball clouds and our route should be clear. We are flying across the state to the International Peace Garden, just north of Dunseith, North Dakota, on the border with Canada. This is an important flight. A necessary flight. We are collecting details.

3.

The International Peace Garden is half in Canada, and half in the United States, but the burger joint is on the American side. Canadians can descend the American steps and order a burger—as long as they go right back to Canada. The hamburger stand offers fries with gravy, something the Canadians appreciate.
—Alton Marsh, "The Nation's Quirkiest Airports," *AOPA Pilot*

4.

Climbing away from the runway, I begin a turn to the left, and Jonathan takes pictures of the fields, the fat green of soybeans, the rich gold of wheat. Some fields appear slate-gray where there is no crop at all, just dirt, because the ground was too wet in the spring for planting. In the language of the Farm Services Agency and crop insurance, the fields themselves "prevented planting." We fly over some of the toughest, wettest soil in the region.

I level the airplane at three thousand feet. According to the instruments, a 20-knot headwind greets us. One hundred and seventy-five nautical miles from the Peace Garden airport, our airspeed is 96 knots. Our ground speed is only 80 knots. It may take us some time to get there, but we should rocket back.

5.

I don't know why we came in second.

The article was titled "The Nation's Quirkiest Airports," but number one looks for aliens more than Cessnas. Named the Greater Green River Intergalactic Spaceport, the Wyoming site has dead animals and parked cars on the deeply rutted runway. Good marketing with the name, perhaps. But nothing more.

The second choice is inspired. An airport set on an international border. An airport in North Dakota! Close enough I could claim it as home territory. An airport where, once landed, a pilot can choose in which country to park his airplane. An airport where they serve french fries with gravy.

I've been to Canada many times. I've been up and down the Alaska highway and the Dempster highway. I've been to Resolute and Grise Fiord, Baffin and Ellesmere Islands, as well as pubs in Ottawa and Montreal. Winnipeg is backyard close. But I've never had french fries with gravy.

Jonathan was born in Williston, just west of the Peace Gardens, and he spent his early youth in Rolla, just east of the Peace Gardens. He has been to the gardens many times. He is mostly vegetarian. But he has never had french fries with gravy. And he has never seen the prairie from only three thousand feet.

Sometimes just a whisper will do. The details are important.

We had to go.

6.

"The river is much better behaved than last time," Jonathan says.

The Red River and the Sheyenne River seem full and fast from the air, their currents inside the treelines of their banks. In truth, however, both still flow above flood stage.

In the fields, the runoff paths make forms that look like the Nazca lines, or cave paintings from La grotte Chauvet-Pont-d'Arc. I see a running deer, perhaps a horse, a standing man with three arms, and then a bear.

7.

"Jon," I say. "If you look out, straight out to the horizon, you'll see two towers. Two radio towers. We are actually lower now than the tops of those towers."

In front of the airplane, the southern tower is directly in our path. Once the tallest structure in the world, the tower rises 2,060 feet off the ground, 3,125 feet above sea level. The Empire State building is only 1,250 feet tall. The Willis Tower, formerly the Sears Tower, in Chicago, is only 1,451 feet tall. In the entire world, only the Burj Khalifa in Dubai is taller, at 2,717 feet.

"Oh," he says, squinting.

"Not seeing it? Really focus on distance. Just a stick up in the sky."

"Nope."

"Oh, well. We'll probably go around it."

8.

Jonathan takes pictures of green fields and yellow fields, tree rows and streams, farmsteads and county roads.

"Does it look like most of the fields have been harvested already?" I ask.

We both peer downward, trying to gauge the height of crops.

"No, it doesn't," he says.

A medical helicopter comes on the radio, departing Fargo for a nearby casualty.

9.

"Jon," I ask, pointing out my side and straight along the wing, "what is that little town right over there?"

Jon looks at his chart and at the moving map in the panel. On the chart, north is up. On the moving map, our direction is up. Jon turns the chart so that it matches the map.

"Page?" he asks.

"Nope. Page is in front of us and off to the left just a bit. What's this one way off to our left?"

"Ayr," he says.

There is a vineyard in Ayr. The Red Trail Vineyard. North Dakota wine. The owners are friends. In an emergency, I think, I could land this plane on the gravel road that runs in front of the store.

"We should go buzz the vineyard," I say.

10.

"Cessna One Two Whiskey," Fargo Departure calls. "Showing light precipitation at ten o'clock to eleven o'clock and four miles, approximately six miles in diameter."

"Roger that, One Two Whiskey," I reply.

Jon and I look out the window and slightly to the left. Gray sky. Ahead and to the right, however, the gray breaks into bright sunshine.

"Do you see the towers yet?" I ask.

"I still see just one," he says.

"Look north."

"Oh," he says, "there it is."

"Can you imagine building that?" I ask. "Can you imagine being this high, exposed and strapped to that thing?"

Jon answers quickly. "No."

11.

"Check this out," I say.

Just south of Galesburg, the land rises into a series of parallel hills that look like rolling waves at sea. Five rolling waves. A section of land cut into thirds, bright dark green then light green then yellow, beans then corn then wheat. Jon hands me the camera and I take a few pictures. I have no idea why the land looks this way.

Valley City is about thirty miles off the left wing. Grand Forks is about forty miles off the right.

"What I cannot get over," I say, "is the history here. We're out of Lake Agassiz, but this is still the Western Interior Seaway. This is still under the ice sheet. This is woolly mammoth and, before that, *T. rex* land. The evidence is everywhere. But it's all so subtle. It's only a hint here, another hint there."

"Did you hear that they are sandbagging in Jamestown?" Jon asks.

The waves recede behind us, and the land flattens out again, deeply puddled and wet.

So many stories, I think.

12.

"I was born in western North Dakota," Jon says, "in Williston, which was the closest hospital to Wild Rose. And only months after I was born we moved to Rolla, North Dakota. I lived there for the first six years of my life, so I don't have very distinct memories, but a lot happened to my family during that time. My sister, who was two years older than me, Deborah was her name, got sick. We all got sick on a family vacation, going to see family in Montana, and the kids all got sick after Christmas, as kids always seem to do. Kind of pneumonia-like, my sister got it worst and it went very quickly, and she died from it. She was three years old and I was one. I have no memory of this, but there are family stories, and I've seen the family movies and pictures of her. She's buried in Rolla. My parents were only thirty-two years old. My father was a pastor, and he had a four-point parish—four churches to serve. The day before I was born, he resigned to take a call to Rolla, just a three-point parish, with Perth and St. John. One of the big things about Rolla besides the death of my sister was the very public grieving because my dad was the pastor. All of the people of the church would come with the theology that "it's God's will," and that just drove my parents nuts. Through a lot of grieving, they challenged that idea of God."

13.

Surrounded by wheat still to be harvested, a radar dome appears in the farmland near Finley. From the old days, I think. It opened in 1952 with a mission to point air force jets toward incoming enemies. From the days when North Dakota held more nuclear missiles than nearly anywhere else on earth and where we imagined a sky with Soviet bombers coming in from the north.

14.

"My dad was born in Coal Harbor, North Dakota," Jon says. "Near Garrison. His family worked on the Garrison Dam. My grandfather had a coal mine for their own personal use up in that area. Kind of a community co-op thing they would do with the coal mine. My mother was practically from North Dakota, but from the Minnesota side of the Red River in Hendrum. And so my father was the poor western North Dakota boy, and my mother was the rich farmer's daughter from the Red River valley. They met at Concordia College."

"What is your earliest memory of living here?" I ask.

"I'm not sure if it's the earliest, but another big moment was building the new church. I remember going up in a cherry picker with the builders when they were completing the steeple. I must have been five years old. I remember going with my mother to Belcourt, on the Indian reservation, where she taught school. And I remember going around the block and collecting ladybugs from the fence."

15.

Midmorning, late summer on a clear day, and no one is working the fields of North Dakota. The morning is too damp, too cloudy, the plants too laden with dew for the combines to roll. Soon, though. I can imagine the farmers standing next to the machines, feeling the air with their faces and breath.

16.

"My father has some good farming stories," Jon says. "He remembers his family homesteaded west river, west of the Missouri, and there were a lot of homesteaders who came, probably more than the land could support with farming. He remembers his main job was moving a lot of rock out of the fields. And when he was twelve, he was driving a tractor on an incline and the tractor tipped over, and his jaw got caught between the wheel and some other part. I can't quite picture it. It really busted up his jaw, and the doctors said he wouldn't live. He had to get his jaw all wired up, and he's only recently been able to open up his mouth with a replacement bridge wide enough to eat tacos or a hamburger."

"He spent his whole life this way?" I ask.

"Yep."

"German immigrants?" I ask.

"His side comes from Russia. Germans from Russia. My great-grandparents came from Russia. The family had been in Russia about 120 years."

17.

We pass white houses and red barns, baseball fields and gravel roads. We pass farm ponds and small lakes. Jonathan takes a fine picture of a flock of swans over water. The sunshine is soft and bright. The fields are all gold and green. We still have a headwind, but only a few small bumps in the air.

18.

On the radio, airplanes report their approaches and landings at the town of Devil's Lake. From three thousand feet, it looks like we are approaching the sea. Devil's Lake, which has no natural outlet, has crested its banks and crossed land to Stump Lake, which drains into the Sheyenne River, which flows into the Red River, which flows into Canada. There is too much water on the plains, and the watersheds are mixing. Ribbons of pavement enter the flood and disappear. Pickup trucks with boat trailers park on county roads at the water's edge. Farmhouses and outbuildings are islands. Treelines bloom green and lush to the shore, then turn to brown sticks in the water. All the small lakes on the northwest side of Devil's Lake have joined as well. Chain

Lake. Mike's Lake. Dry Lake. Morrison Lake. Sweetwater Lake. There is no shore, no separation, no difference.

Hydrologists call it a wet cycle. Other people call it a disaster.

"I always wondered how the town of Churchs Ferry got its name," Jon says.

19.

In the distance, white spires rise from the green fields north of Rugby, the blades of each wind turbine turning slowly in the air. It's like watching a dance, I think. A stately, old-fashioned waltz, perhaps. Everything measured and timed and graceful and fluid. Bright-blue cloudless sky behind them. I do not know why, but the windmill, in all its forms, seems right to me. A fine transition from one form of movement to another. No harm. No waste. Full beauty.

20.

"When I was in college," Jon says, "I was part of an organization called Bread and Cheese. It was an antiwar, antinuclear group. We'd gather every first Wednesday of the month when the alert sirens were tested, and we'd have signs that said, 'Silence the Sirens.' We'd have a silent vigil then, too. One time we went up with this antinuclear peace group and camped out at the missile silos. This was in the '80s when Reagan was really building up the nuclear missile–silo program. So we each in small groups went out and camped overnight just outside the fence around the silo. The one I went to was not far from Grand Forks."

21.

"Supposedly," I say, "we are getting close to the Turtle Mountains. Not many mountains, though."

"Turtles," Jon says, smiling, "are not very tall."

22.

Fifteen miles from the Peace Garden airport, I begin to self-announce on the radio. There is no other traffic on the radio. It seems there is no other traffic in the air. We approach the 100th meridian, the line every geography student learns is the divider between the moist East and the arid West, and the land below us changes from prairie farmland to forest, deep and large forest, running north and west. Smoke rises from two treelines to the north, some small portion of the forest on fire. We fly over haystacks in mown fields and cattle in pastureland.

Another voice comes on the radio. "Inbound aircraft, do you require US or Canadian customs?"

This is not a question I've ever been asked before.

"US," I say, guessing.

The man does not reply.

"Do we need customs?" Jon asks.

"Hell, I don't know," I say. "Someone may meet us. Did you bring your passport?"

"Yes," he says. "You?"

"No."

23.

The approach to the airport is very pretty. A small lake. Bales of hay. Forest, then, and rolling hills. The airplane touches down easily, and we taxi to the west end, then turn to the American side of the ramp. No one comes out of any building. We shut down, get out of the airplane, shut the doors, and walk to a set of steps that lead to the gardens. No customs official meets us. At the entrance sign, we take a picture of a woman from South Dakota, and she takes a picture of us. I step into Canada, step back, step into Canada again, then go for it fully.

I admit I did not come here for the flowers, but the flowers are impressive. I do not know their names, but white and red and blue and purple and green flowers in neatly ordered beds under a warm blue sky with small white clouds slow everyone's walking pace. This is a place for strolling. A sign embedded in a rock monument near the entrance reads, "To God in His Glory, We Two Nations Dedicate This Garden and Pledge Ourselves That as Long as Men Shall Live, We Will Not Take Up Arms against One Another."

Seems like a good idea to me.

Jon and I walk westward, through the flower gardens, over a grassy central path, around pools with fountains. We pass small posts with the phrase "May Peace Prevail on Earth" written in a different language on each side. There are seven posts. Twenty-eight languages. We pass a bell tower, the Peace Tower, and a monument for 9/11 with pieces of the World Trade Center. We open a gate and go through an inner garden to make our way to the café.

This is it, I think, the whole reason we are here.

At the counter, I order a cheeseburger, then french fries with gravy.

"Poutine?" the man asks.

I have no idea what he means.

"Sure," I say.

24.

The waitress looks a bit surprised. Holding the two plates, she says, "These are *both* for you?"

25.

One of my favorite quotes:

Exploration is the physical expression of the Intellectual Passion.

And I tell you, if you have the desire for knowledge and the power to give it physical expression, go out and explore. If you are a brave man you will do nothing: if you are fearful you may do much, for none but cowards have need to prove their bravery. Some will tell you that you are mad, and nearly all will say, "What is the use?" For we are a nation of shopkeepers, and no shopkeeper will look at research which does not promise him a financial return within a year. And so you sledge nearly alone, but those with whom you sledge will not be shopkeepers: that is worth a good deal. If you march your Winter Journeys you will have your reward, so long as all you want is a penguin's egg.

—Apsley Cherry-Garrard, *The Worst Journey in the World*

26.

Sometimes all it takes is a whisper. A sound, a sight, an idea can create a desire to go.

All I wanted was french fries with gravy. I've learned its name, poutine, and I've heard it described at a heart attack in a bowl. French fries, cheese curds, strong brown chicken gravy—the idea of it is strong enough to clog the arteries. The taste of it is strong enough to forgive the sin.

The details are important. It doesn't matter if they don't make something larger or deep. Each one is a seed. It may take years before they find their own place to grow.

On the way back to the airplane, a customs official comes out and stops us by the stairs. He asks for identification, then asks where I was born. Just routine. He tells us there is a logbook to sign at the airplane ramp, and when we get there we find a jar duct-taped to the airport sign. Inside the jar is a small notebook. There is only one other entry: from January.

The Beautiful Line

Tell me about the beginning of desire.

We hear a story, or a question, or a challenge, someone else's adventure—someone we know or someone so deep in a history even Marco Polo would find ancient—and that story lingers. It settles in and finds a home. It *abides* in us. In the deepest and most gut-true sense, it simply won't go away. We want that story. Someone has crossed a line on the earth or in the heart. Me too, we think. Somehow different and somehow better. But always me too.

If not me *too,* then me *first.*

I wish I could tell you when this story begins. Perhaps the honest beginning would be the moment some hominoid from the Olduvai Gorge first reached a hilltop and thought, however dimly, *I wonder what would happen if I just kept going*—and then kept going. He or she crossed a line. Not a line in rock or forest or dirt. A line in courage. A line in experience and imagination.

In my own life, an article in *National Geographic* would be a safe bet. Or some adventure printed on laminated SRA cards in my third-grade schoolroom. To cross a border. To be someplace else. Someplace with deep history. Someplace where the rocks were nearly luminous with the evidence of story. To find the size and shape of the earth and feel the limits of it all in my boots. In a personal way, to own. But so much more. To find all the old boundaries broken or exceeded. To face a world more exotic than fanciful, more real than simply imagined. To see the idea of a planet made specific and detailed and to make the examples intimate.

Not to see everything, but to know how big that everything is.

To the east—
Black Bear. Timber Wolf. Moose.

To the west—
Bison. Prairie Dog. Elk.

I could tell you the story began when the ideas of *place* and *history* and *story* first joined in some early human brain. I could tell you the story begins when a child first places a finger against a globe and gives the thing a spin. I could tell you the story begins when a teacher first speaks the name Magellan. Each claim would be true. Each claim would be limited, though, and false. This story is everywhere and in everything. Where, the physicists ask, is the edge of the universe? What is its size? And if we cannot measure it in light-years, can we measure it in dimensions beyond the three we touch?

All we want is a border, an edge. Something to see and then to cross.

To the east—
Voyageurs and Vikings.
To the west—
Lewis and Clark.

"Cessna One Zero Eight Nine Seven, cleared for takeoff."

"Cleared for takeoff, Eight Nine Seven," I reply.

The throttle goes in again. The airplane rolls, then rushes, then lifts itself into the sky.

Such a beautiful day for flying! Every field is green. Lush green. Ireland green. Corn and sugar beets and soybeans. A few fields of yellow just to make the landscape pop. Harvested wheat, I think. High-contrast color on the flat-land prairie.

Three thousand feet above sea level and heading northeast toward the town of Twin Valley, I am looking for a border. Subtle, yes. But real and demanding. No gates or crossing guards. No pole dropped across a roadway. Just a shift in the ground where everything changes.

I am looking for the beginning of the American prairie.

Underneath the wings, though, now the squares of sectioned land. Roads run ruler straight either north and south or east and west. Intersections every mile. At farmsteads, shelterbelts line the roadways and run just as straight, every tree imported from some other place. Cropland, every quarter-section tilled and planted. Only a railway has the bravado to angle its way from one horizon to the other. Only a stream has the turns and curves of something less and more than planned. It's a stunning sight, if only for the size of the work.

Near Twin Valley, however, this all should change.

Change perspective and the borders change with you.

Two o'clock and I am sitting at Taiwhanga o paneke, the Wellington Foyer of the Te Papa Museum in Wellington, New Zealand, after the long overnight flight into Auckland and then the predawn jump down the island. Jet-lagged and coffee-buzzed, I am already facing the Void. That's what the sign says. The Void.

Just outside the Void, I am watching groups of uniformed schoolchildren, senior citizens, couples hand in hand. Everyone rushes. Everyone is happy. Te Papa is a national museum and a good one. Five floors of geography, culture, history, everything from immigration stories to refugee stories to the geology of the place and its physical history from Gondwanaland to today. Changing ideas about agriculture. Interactive rooms for children. A marae. Pictures of the homes and villages hammered by the Mount Tarawera volcanic explosion in 1886. A thousand artifacts behind glass. Movies that present the creation myths. The Treaty of Waitangi on large display boards in both English and Maori. A giant squid, in the flesh and under glass. A 3-D movie showing what life must be like in the deep ocean for the squid.

Like all wonderful museums, it's also a bit self-defeating in that it's overwhelming. Any one hall is the result of countless years of countless people's study and passion. We stroll through the halls, the displays, and examine each artifact casually at a tourist's pace, and with luck the most we understand is that there is this whole huge thing called history. Somehow we are part of this, but then there are also those wonderful birds hovering on the wind outside the window and the peculiarly beautiful way the light reflects off the harbor water.

People walk straight into the Void, pause, look down and then up, gasp or smile or reach for some balance.

"This is so cool!" a young boy says to a friend.

It's called Te Kore. The Void. Two black disks, one on the floor and one in the ceiling five floors above, the space between them open and empty. Cool white neon circles the disk on the floor and intersects the disk in the ceiling. On a sign I read that this represents the space before creation. An endlessly and infinitely creative space. *Ihonui,* or core. Sitting just outside the circles, I am amazed at the way empty space can stop a body in motion. People walk into the Void, on their way to some other exhibit or wing, not paying any attention at all to where they are, and then suddenly they stop—the openness above them calling to something else in their body. They look up, at one black circle, then down at their feet and the other circle. What in the world is *this,* they wonder. And then they smile. The space *before* anything else. Ohhhh, they seem to say. Always wondered about that.

To the east—
26.36 inches of rain each year. Twenty-five tornadoes.
To the west—
15.36 inches of rain each year. Twenty-two tornadoes.

Beyond the Void, behind a wall, in an exhibit called *Our Space*, a fourteen-meter-long image of New Zealand is set into the floor, a mosaic of fused satellite color images and an interactive display. The room is dark, and the image is lit from below. The whole floor glows.

People stand on the map, and monitors in the walls come to light to show scenes and stories about the place where they stand. But no one pays any attention to the scenes of children or farming or history. No one pays any attention to the wall at all. Everyone points at the map, squats down, traces their fingers down roads or valleys or along waterways and bays and rivers. Children get down on hands and knees, lower their faces nearly to the glass, trying to find a home or school or whatever they want to see. This is where, they say. This is where I live. This is where I work. This is where I go to school. This is where we got married. This is where we went hiking. All the borders of time and money and geography and history are gone. This is where.

Sometimes the children stomp about like mile-high monsters, laughing, smashing their towns and roaring like Godzilla. Sometimes they get protective and won't let anyone stand on their house.

On the far side of the Void, I wonder about the perspective. We are walking over the landscape like God. Not one person looks to the walls or listens to the soft recorded voices explaining where we are. Everyone is mindful where they step. Some people seem to take up a position and stand still, surveying the world before them, joining this place and that place in their mind's eye from this altitude. Others nearly run from one spot to another. Eventually, every single person points at something, at some place. Here and here and here and here, they say.

I will find out later that the photography is from the Landsat 5 satellite, 705 kilometers above the surface of the earth, and the scale of the map is 1:113,000. We are giants in this room! We are 438 miles tall. And there isn't a cloud in the sky.

What I see most clearly, though, is that this perspective, this freedom, brings joy. Everyone has their own stories. Where they live, where they are going, what they have seen, what they have heard. "Where is . . . ?" is the question I hear over and over. Friends and family members confer and walk around to find it out. Finally, it all fits together, the way this river comes from this mountain and flows past this town and enters into the ocean. I have been to parts of this story, people say. And now I see the whole thing. This is the place where I have been, where I will be, where I am from—all of it.

This is the place where I will be. You have to cross the Void to get here. You have to cross the Void to get back.

To the east—
Ojibwe. Chippewa.
To the west—
Mandan. Hidatsa. Arikara. Assiniboine. Lakota. Dakota.

A line is a way to divide. A line is also a way to see.

Lake Agassiz had a beach. In the days of mammoths and mastodons, sandy and rolling dunes fronted the glacier-melt water. When the water receded, dragging icebergs through the lake-bottom silt, the beach ridges remained. Find a map of the American prairie, and you will see the beach line east of the North Dakota border with Minnesota. To the east, a deciduous biome. Farther east, a coniferous biome. To the west, the tallgrass prairie. Farther west, mixed grass, then short grass. The American steppe.

I have seen this change a thousand times on the ground, my Jeep speeding through heat wave or blizzard, but only so far as a groundling can see. What I want to see today is more of this line. I want to see the behavior of the earth change from one thing to another. I want to follow this line and take its measure. On the ground, I want to know what I see and touch is a part of something large and historic.

The airplane is easy in the sky today. The wind, 20 knots from the west at this altitude, is steady and invisible. It's too early for thermals, and the air is smooth.

I am looking for the difference. I am looking for the change in the landscape, the change in the trees.

"Cessna Eight Nine Seven," Fargo Departure calls. "Leaving the Fargo TRSA, radar service terminated. Squawk VFR. Frequency change approved. Good morning."

On a radar screen inside the Fargo control tower, there is a ring that shows a distance thirty miles from the airfield. Inside this line, air traffic control keeps track of the airplanes and keeps us apart. Outside the line, we're a good bit more on our own. Inside the line, I am required to listen to the assigned radio frequencies. Outside the line, I don't have to listen at all. I am about to cross the border of their responsibility. In truth, I crossed this line nearly fifteen miles back. Because of my altitude, I am technically underneath the area of their concern. In practice, however, once inside the outer line, you're inside the TRSA. But I am not leaving.

"Fargo approach, I'm going to be turning south and staying inside the TRSA for another ten or fifteen minutes," I say.

"Cessna Eight Nine Seven, roger. You're going to be turning southbound at this time?"

"In about two minutes, yes, sir. Eight Nine Seven," I say.

"Cessna Eight Nine Seven, roger. I'll keep you for TRSA service then."

Outside the airplane, I can see a treeline approaching. Not a shelterbelt. Not riparian trees along some stream. This is forestland. On the airplane's moving map I can see the same TRSA line they see inside the control tower. The trees come right up to the edge. I put the airplane on the inside of the curved line and begin to fly that arc, like a child trailing a stick along a chain-link fence, ready to light out for the territory at any moment.

To the east—
Garrison Keillor.
To the west—
Theodore Roosevelt.

A map is a collection of borders. A hiker will show you a topographical map, contour lines showing the borders of elevation. A social scientist will show you a map that divides a town into sections where people have more or fewer college degrees, more or fewer magazine subscriptions, more or fewer pieces of NASCAR clothing. Politicians redraw the boundaries of their districts to better represent their people, or get reelected. At the Centers for Disease Control, there are maps that show who a future pandemic will kill first, then who will die on day two.

When the borders move, we cannot help but watch. A blue line moves across our television as a cold front drops out of Montana and freezes Nebraska. A thick black line on the newsreel map expands as the Allied forces move inland from Normandy. A bandanna, tied to a rope and suspended over a puddle of mud, moves toward the winners in tug-of-war. Every border implies a question: where are you? Which side are you on? Imagine you are there. Every border, then, is a moment of self-evaluation and self-discovery. I am here.

There is a GPS moving map in the airplane's panel. It shows me the world underneath the wings. It shows me radio towers I need to avoid. It shows me the names of lakes and streams and highways and towns. It shows me the weather, too. I can move a small pointer, and the screen will tell me the radio frequencies of distant airports. It tells me what I need to be safe.

I can change the range of this map, from very close, just the airplane sitting on a taxiway, to all of North America. But it will not show me history. We've all seen Pangaea and Gondwanaland break up and move apart, to form the continents we know. But those movies show the continents in their current form. I want to see Lake Agassiz. I want to see the Interior Seaway. I want to see the Laurentide ice sheet advance and get split by the Coteau des Prairies. I want to see the waters of Lake Agassiz rolling onto the beach ridge that passes underneath this airplane. I want to see a Mars-size something hit the still-forming earth and form the moon. I want to see the asteroid that made the Manson Crater, and the one that fell on the Yucatán. I know the land can rise and fall, the inhalations and exhalations of a planet, and I want to see this planet take that breath.

South of Twin Valley, there is a swirl in the land. I can see a long arc, a little bit of rising, a little bit of change in elevation. It looks exactly like someone placed a very large paintbrush on the earth and gave it a twist. Brush lines in the dirt. But this is no farmer's art. It's big, and I have no idea what it is or how it got here. The fields are still very green. There are more trees now. In front of me I see forest and then lakes. The map gives them names. Union Lake, Maple Lake, White Earth Lake, South Twin Lake, Bass Lake. Perhaps it's just the angle of sunlight this morning, but heading east I could not see the shift in the land. Now that I'm turning south, I can see the hills and bluffs. I can begin to see the shore.

I have been in the forests, and I have been on the prairie. What I have never done is follow the space where they meet. I want to trace the beautiful line. At altitude, where all the patterns shift, I want to be *between* the things I know.

A new controller comes on the radio. "Cessna Eight Nine Seven," she says, "you left the Fargo TRSA. Radar service terminated. Squawk VFR. Frequency change approved. You can give me a call when you're back in."

I've been flying the edge of their yard, I think. I've been tight-roping their border. I've been causing them to pay more attention to where I am than I should. In or out, they say. In or out. Either cross this border or don't, but don't just sit on the line.

"Going VFR, Eight Nine Seven. Thank you," I say.

To the east—
Paul Bunyan.
To the west—
Sitting Bull.

When similarity-biased regionalizations are mapped, however, the map reader sees not only the area-shading or alphameric symbols used to distinguish the regions; he also is confronted by the boundaries between these regions. How a person interprets a map is far from being clearly understood, but it is believed that a map reader attaches some significance to these boundary lines themselves. (Note: Jenks and Caspall suggest that map readers attempt to extract from a map one or a combination of three facets of the distribution: the overview of general trends, the data values for specific places, and the boundary lines between patterns. These authors hold that these boundaries are compared with mental images of other aspects of the area mapped.)

—Mark Monmonier, *Maximum-Difference Barriers:*
An Alternative Numerical Regionalization Method

The town of Ulen off to my right. The town of Waubun coming up on my left. Ogema and Hitterdal also in view. Farm ponds reflect the sky. High clouds and haze. You can see why birds fly into windows—that clear reflection masking the hard and bone-shattering border. It's a wonder they don't fly into lakes.

In the eastern distance, I can see a rise to the land. I can even see a bump on the horizon that's not a cloud. No farmers work the fields today. This is late July. What's done is done. Harvest is next.

What I see approaching the airplane is a line of trees, a hard and clear edge to a forest. On the ground here the folding of the earth, the rises and ravines, frames the eyesight. A bit west, the frame is simply the horizon, endless distance to outer space. I make a note that from the air, the subtle change to the topography is not quite as visible. Instead, water and wood, isolated to the ground view, appear with the force of huge territory. But no sooner than I make this note I am proven wrong. I look straight down instead of toward the land in front of me, and I see hills and valleys. I see where water has moved the soil. I see hilltop crops bend in the wind.

If it is possible to be directly over the beach, I am over it now. To my right there is nothing but farmland, sectioned and ordered. The only trees are those built to protect a building or field. To my left there is nothing but forest and lakes. I take a picture first one way and then the other. The change is as fast as the wings are wide.

To my left—

To my right—

Given the strengths of all boundaries between pairs of adjacent OTUs [operational taxonomic units], a technique is needed for consistently selecting a string of boundaries to form a barrier between high-order regions. Two considerations are important. First, all boundaries forming the barrier must be linked together and must either form a closed loop or have both ends terminate at the edge of the study area or against another barrier. Second, the most important barrier should contain the boundary with the steepest gradient.

—Mark Monmonier, *Maximum-Difference Barriers:*
An Alternative Numerical Regionalization Method

People have died because of borders. Israel. Africa. India. Europe. The United States. Which side of the line is your home? The maximum difference is seldom geographic. Homeland is history.

Seven miles north of the town of Lake Park, I can see Upper Cormorant Lake, Floyd Lake, and I wonder why we don't name open land. We name lakes. We name forests. Can we name a place without a border?

I can see Detroit Lake in the distance. The treeline dodges from there to here. Below me, silver grain bins and silos. Red barns. Green fields. Hilly land. I cross Highway 10 between Lake Park and Hawley, and everything south and east of Hawley is different. Suddenly, the land is just lake after lake after lake. Minnesota claims ten thousand lakes. In fact, there are many more. Forest between them all. The land is not mountain dramatic, but it is no longer flat or open, either. I have crossed the line again, and the prairie is behind me.

Dear Scott,
Maximum distance refers to "distance" measured using a variety of criteria, not just the two or three we commonly use—think of a set of data with multiple measurements for socioeconomic conditions (various measures describing how the populations of census tracts or counties differ in age, sex, race, education, income, employment, etc.). The algorithm looks at the distance (or difference) between census tracts or counties that share a common boundary. Unless the two are identical, there is some distance (or difference). The idea is to draw a boundary that splits the region into two parts, and to do this so that there is a relatively high distance (or difference) along the entire boundary. After drawing one boundary that splits the region into two parts, the algorithm might (if asked) find a second high-contrast boundary that partitions one of these first two parts
Mark

I like the idea of maximum difference. My camera does not do it justice. To my left, hills you can hide behind. To my right, the exposure of the prairie. In front and above me, the clouds are high and thin. There is no front in the air today, at least not here, but there are borders of sunlight and shadow on the ground.

I cross the Ottertail River. Lake Traverse is thirty miles in front of me and Big Stone Lake just beyond that. Both of them narrow and long, they seem unremarkable. But a continental divide separates them. On one side of the line, water heads toward Hudson Bay. On the other side, water heads for the Gulf of Mexico. Their history is huge.

It's called the Traverse Gap, a valley with a continental divide. Pleistocene Lake Agassiz was dammed up on the south end by the Big Stone Moraine and stoppered on the north side by the Laurentide ice. For whatever reason, the water breached the moraine about 11,700 years ago and created a spillway, which became a torrent, which became enormous and hard. Glacial River Warren carved the valleys of the Minnesota and Upper Mississippi Rivers. Then the lake opened on the north, and the river dried up. The spillway gorge became the gap. You cannot see the Continental Divide from the air. But you can see Traverse Lake. You can see Big Stone Lake to the south. And you can see the cut in the earth between them.

Flying nearly down the line between sunlight and shadow, I am flying down the middle of the lakes as well. When I cross the gap, I turn for home.

We have all tried to do it—walk a straight line. We've put our feet on a board, a line in a sidewalk, a rope in the air, and done our best to keep right above it. The thrill is the potential fall one way or the other. Every muscle in our body tenses and works toward balance. It's damn difficult. Failure is expected. Success brings joy. If we get across the space, it would be wrong to say we've gained both sides. We have moved *between* them. We have avoided either definition. We know there is more space between atoms than there are atoms, but we haven't figured out how to go there yet. So perhaps our love of the beautiful line is a way to say *both* as well as *neither* at the same time.

An ecologist would tell you that the line of maximum difference is also the place of maximum diversity. Timber wolf meets bison, introduced by coyote. The border is a mixing place. Think tide pools at the ocean shore. Think atmosphere above a planet. Think the euphotic zone at sea.

So here is a truth about the beautiful line. The border is the place where the world gets creative. How do I get across? What has changed? To see both sides is to understand them both more deeply. And let's face it—every border invites transgression.

At the edge of the forest, every animal wonders.

Acknowledgments

This book benefits from the knowledge, patience, goodwill, great humor, and support of many people and organizations. Concordia College in Moorhead, Minnesota, where I teach, has been extraordinary with their support. The Minnesota States Arts Board and the North Dakota Institute for Regional Studies contributed significant funds that allowed me to rent an airplane and go exploring. The USGS, NOAA, the Grand Forks office of the National Weather Service, the North Dakota Geological Survey, and the Army Corps of Engineers never failed to provide help or answer questions. The Canon Camera Company lent me a very nice compact camera that took most of the photographs in this book.

There are people who deserve special mention because they either opened doors to information for me or suffered through early drafts of these chapters. Peter Chilson, Elizabeth Dodd, Joel Orth, Mike Paulson, Paul Seifert, Heidi Manning, Shawn Dobberstein, Daryl Ritchison, Mark Ewens, Dan Ehlen, Pat Valdata, Rich Schueneman, Fred Remer, and Fred J. Anderson all have my deep and heartfelt thanks.

A number of the chapters in this book first appeared as essays in various magazines, sometimes in slightly revised form. My thanks to each of these journals and their editors:

Air Facts—"Storm Flying"

Alaska Quarterly Review—"Walking Chaucer"

AOPA Flight Training—"Short-Hop Notebook: Math Class," "Short-Hop Notebook: The Swoop"

AOPA Pilot—"That Thing Up Front"

Kenyon Review On-line—"The Beautiful Line"

KinshipofRivers.org—"River Flying: The Red River"
South Dakota Review and *About Place: Trees*—"A Wall of Old Trees"
St. Katherine Review—"Thin Places and Thick Time: A Duet for Two Worlds"
Tampa Review—"Tag"
Terrain.org—"River Flying: The Sheyenne River"

Illustration Credits

Unless otherwise noted, photos by author.

A Wall of Old Trees
Shelterbelt maps, 1936, National Forest Service, courtesy of Joel Orth

River Flying: The Red River
Photos by Jonathan Steinwand

Ground Reference
Detail, "Mountain on the Prairie," Lewis and Clark map, courtesy of Library of Congress

Isostatic gravity anomaly map and aeromagnetic anomaly map, courtesy of U.S. Geological Survey, U.S. Department of the Interior

Sectional maps by author using FalconView, open-source Wiki

Radar image, NEXRAD, courtesy of National Weather Service

Very Deep Low
October 2010 windstorm map, surface analysis map, and satellite image of Earth, courtesy of National Oceanic and Atmospheric Administration, National Weather Service

Deep SWE
2011 snow survey photos, courtesy of National Operational Hydrologic Remote Sensing Center, National Oceanic and Atmospheric Administration, National Weather Service

About the Author

W. Scott Olsen teaches at Concordia College in Moorhead, Minnesota, where he also edits the literary magazine *Ascent.* He is the author of numerous books, including *Never Land: Adventures, Wonder, and One World Record in a Very Small Plane* and *Hard Air: Adventures from the Edge of Flying.*

Photo by Matt Randle